"Cheapskate Living And Loving It" ·

Chapter 1

Saving Money on Your Grocery Bill

Groceries are one in every of the biggest payments that lots of us need to finances for every month. It isn't a luxurious object that we are able to pick out to stay without, however there are lots of approaches with a view to shop in your grocery invoice every week!

1. Start clipping coupons. Every 12 months organizations ship out hundreds of thousands of greenbacks really well worth of coupons, however most effective a fragment of them are used. If you're taking simply one hour every week and begin clipping coupons, you may locate that you'll be capin a position to shop for call logo ingredients for plenty inexpensive than you'll pay for

even the shop brands. At first, that is going to price you some greenbacks in keeping with week however ultimately it's far going to repay substantially.

Now, I need to provide an explanation for that in conjunction with our meals we generally buy
our family materials in addition to our toiletries, so this is going to be a part of what you may shop cash on with coupons.

The first factor you will do is to accumulate your coupons. You can print those offline or clip them from your Sunday paper. There are even webweb sites on line wherein you should buy inserts for as little as 25 cents every plus shipping. This makes it lots inexpensive than shopping for a Sunday paper, which generally runs approximately $2.50 on average.

If you've got got a huge own circle of relatives to feed, you'll be capable of buy more than one inserts to prevent a ton of cash. Now, many humans will clip some coupons and exit to the neighborhood save and use them proper away. You aren't going to do that. You are going to shop your coupons for whilst there's a sale and inventory up on that object at no cost or nearly free.

You want to inventory up sufficient of that object to get you via approximately 6 weeks, that is whilst the object will move on sale again. Here is an instance this is the usage of hygiene products, there has been a selected logo call shampoo and conditioner that became on sale at my neighborhood save. The ordinary rate became $three.50 in keeping with bottle however it became on sale for $2.50 a bottle.

I knew I had ten $five off bottle coupons, so I ended up getting 10 shampoos and 10 conditioners clearly free. Another one which I simply took benefit of became a completely pricey lotion that became on sale at my save for $three.00 in keeping with bottle. I had ten
$five off coupons which made them 50 cents a piece, however to pinnacle that off I had a discount that gave me $five off a buy of
$25 or extra making 20 creams clearly free!

You can do that on meals much like you could on frame products, cleansing products, and laundry materials. Wait for a sale, pinnacle it with a discount and get the bottom rate possible!

2. Grocery keep at your neighborhood greenback save. I am speakme approximately your greenback save that sells the entirety for a greenback! They promote groceries there too. They additionally take coupons, which makes the entirety very cheap. For instance, they promote cereal at my neighborhood greenback save. Cereal for a greenback is great, however throw a discount on pinnacle of that and get it for sixty six cents a box, now this is amazing!

3. Plan your food every week and use your grocery save flyer to do so! Every week you have to get your grocery save flyer withinside the mail, use this in conjunction with your coupons to determine what you will consume for the week. Write down all of the elements you may want for you food making plans them round what's on sale.

4. Shop on your very own pantry. This is a huge one! So commonly

humans do now no longer comprehend what they sincerely have of their cabinets. Have you ever went to the shop, noticed some thing you concept you needed, offered it most effective to return back domestic and locate three of the precise equal untouched product on your cabinet? Once you've got got created your

listing of all of the elements you may want for the week, take a look at your pantry to look when you have any of them already in there.

5. Cook once, consume 3 times. This is one in every of my favorites. Did you already know that you can sincerely get 3 food for a own circle of relatives of 4 out of simply one chook? This is how I do it; first, I boil the split chook to make chook and dumplings with. I put off all the beef from the bones after the chook has boiled; use the inventory to make my dumplings including approximately 1/three of the beef. Then, I positioned the bones and pores and skin withinside the crock-pot to make chook noodle soup inventory. Finally, I am capable of throw a few fish fry sauce at the 2/three chook meat I actually have left and serve barbequed chook sandwiches.

You can do that with lots of various ingredients and reduce lower back on what you're procuring meat every week!

6. Find a neighborhood cut price grocery keep. Many human beings like to mention that the meals you're shopping for at a reduction grocery keep isn't anyt any correct and you may get unwell in case you consume it. That in reality isn't always true. Each week I load up my kids and force 50 miles to the nearest cut price grocery keep. The purpose is that I am capable of actually triple my cash I even have budgeted for groceries. For example, I am capin a position to shop for entire frozen natural chickens for no extra than $3. Now I even have instructed you the way we are able to make one fowl ultimate 3 days, so it's miles costing me $1 an afternoon for our fowl!

You should buy the whole thing you want at a reduction grocery keep! They promote milk manner less expensive than you may ever discover on the grocery keep and it isn't always out of date. They promote a 24 case of yogurt for two bucks! Check round and spot when you have a reduction grocery keep close to you, even when you have to force a bit ways, it's miles really well worth it due to the fact you'll be saving extra than you could believe in your grocery invoice.

7. So often, we've leftovers after dinner and assume not anything approximately throwing them withinside the trash. If you really need to keep cash, you want to reconsider leftovers. Make them into some thing different, take them for lunch tomorrow study the ones leftovers as your cash, don ' t throw your cash away. There are even instances I purposely make leftovers due to the fact I recognize we are able to consume it on some other night time or I plan to make it into some thing else. Another splendid aspect my children like to do is leftover day. We keep what's leftover in the course of the week, throw it withinside the freezer, then on Sunday have a buffet kind meal with all forms of choices. This guarantees not anything is going to waste.

8. Stop snacking or permitting kids to graze at the same time as they're at home. So a good deal meals can disappear in case you permit your kids to get withinside the pantry and consume every time they sense like it. You want to installation a time table due to the fact the reality is that kids in addition to many adults will consume virtually due to the fact the meals is there and that they can.

9. Set a finances and persist with it. If you place a finances and persist with it you may research in no time the way to stretch you cash. I am now no longer joking once I say persist with it. If you buy groceries on Saturdays and run out of meals on Thursday, you may discover ways to stretch anything is left to your shelves and you'll be a good deal extra careful the subsequent week.

10. Only visit the shop as soon as every week and go together with a listing. Never cross in the shop with out a listing of the objects you propose to shop for. If you do, you may discover

which you are over spending and now no longer getting the meals which you really want to put together food with. Take your listing and don't permit temptation to overhaul you. Never visit the shop simply to choose up one or matters as soon as you've got got already carried out your weekly shopping. So often, we cross in seeking out one or objects and pop out with a cartload. If you neglect about some thing, make due or parent some thing else out, however do now no longer cross again into that keep. If you surely must cross in, simplest take the quantity of

cash had to buy the object you want. Leave the debit card withinside the vehicle and clutch a bit cash.

Chapter 2

Saving Money on Your Electric Bill

Oh how we dread considering electric powered invoice every and each month. There was instances that I had no concept how a good deal power I had used and felt absolutely helpless. That turned into till I obtained an electric powered invoice that turned into extra than my residence price ultimate winter. I determined matters needed to change. Here are a few adjustments you could make.

1. No extra dryer! Did you already know that you can decrease your

electric powered invoice noticeably in case you simply prevent the usage of your dryer? In the spring, summer time season and maximum of the autumn you could line dry your garments outside. In the winter, you should buy a cheap (normally round $5) drying rack in your residence. These racks normally preserve approximately one load of laundry every.

2. How often have we been instructed that we have to flip the warmth down in our houses if we need to decrease our electric powered invoice? I turned into

   Taught which you ought to flip it down, then in case you get clearly bloodless, heat up the residence and flip it back off again. Then a study came out by my local electric company that said do not set your thermostat at one temperature and leave it there unless you are going to be out of the house for several hours or are going to bed. What you could do is withinside the wintry weather begin together along with your thermostat at sixty eight ranges, in case you are cushty at that temperature drop it to 67. Continue to do that till you discover the temperature which you simply can not stand. In my residence, we regularly have jackets, more than one layers or blankets on us withinside the wintertime.

In the summer time season, you need to do the opposite. Set your thermostat at seventy four ranges and spot how heat you could stand it. On the times that it isn't extraordinarily warm, open your home windows, switch on the lovers and permit the summer time season air in your private home. Most of the time for the duration of the spring and fall you ought to permit your home windows to be open because the temperature out of doors isn't too warm or too bloodless.

3. Check all your home windows and doorways for gaps in addition to round your baseboards when you have a basement. In older homes, that is wherein quite a few warmness is misplaced and bloodless air is available in at. If you discover gaps, restoration them.

4. Close off the rooms that aren't in use. Shut the doorways to the

rooms that no person is in. If the youngsters are withinside the dwelling room, there's no purpose to warmness the bedrooms. If no person is withinside the bathroom, close that door. This will maintain the bulk of the warmth withinside the foremost a part of the residence close to the thermostat, on the way to make sure your furnace isn't over operating and also you aren't losing any warmness. You can do the equal issue withinside the summer time season!

5. Open your curtains withinside the wintry weather and near them withinside the summer time season! Find the home windows in your private home that face the solar, whilst the solar is excessive withinside the sky, open the ones curtains withinside the wintry weather, this may help

warmness your property. In the summer time season, it's going to warmness your property as properly so ensure you shut up the curtains.

6. Unplug everything! Did you realize that even as you sleep at night time and all your electronics are close off, they're nonetheless the usage of energy? Even that mobileular telecellsmartphone charger you depart plugged into the wall whilst your telecellsmartphone isn't charging is continuously the usage of energy. When you end the usage of some thing, unplug it.

7. Wash your garments in bloodless water. This will paintings for almost all of people, until you've got got an incredibly grimy task you ought to wash all your garments in bloodless water. If you've got got garments which are very soiled, you ought to maintain them cut loose the relaxation of your apparel and wash them in warm water with the aid of using themselves. You ought to additionally ensure to clean your whites in warm water as a minimum as soon as in line with month to make sure they live brilliant white.

8. Remove a number of the mild bulbs! In my residence, I even have chandeliers that dangle from the ceiling, every of those takes 8 mild bulbs. In no manner will we want 8 mild bulbs to mild our rooms, so I best placed mild bulbs in every one. True it does now no longer have the equal impact as all 8, however you'll keep cash in case you don't top off your mild fixtures.

9. Change your filters to your furnace/air conditioner each month to

maintain it from over operating and to maintain the air flowing.

10. If you've got got the selection among the microwave oven and your traditional oven, use the microwave, it makes use of ninety percentage much less energy than the traditional oven. If you need to use the traditional oven open it up after you close up if off withinside the wintry weather, you could use that warmness this is trapped in there to heat your property.

Chapter 3

Television, Phone, Internet, Cells and More

I as soon as observed myself paying over $a hundred for my satellite tv for pc invoice, $70 for my internet, $60 for a domestic telecellsmartphone and over $a hundred a month for my mobileular telecellsmartphone. I turned into bored with losing cash on those things, so I made some changes. Here are some guidelines for you for saving cash on those payments and more!

1. Cut out the satellite tv for pc. There isn't anyt any purpose which

will pay that big satellite tv for pc invoice every month, rather choose Netflix or some thing like Netflix. Today there are heaps of various applications you could pick from and that they begin at about $7 a month. Sure, you'll be one season at the back of at the suggests you watch, however clearly what does that

count whilst you are saving over $1,000 a year!

Instead of the use of the video on call for service, wait and watch the film later. There isn't anyt any factor in paying $five to observe a film once, whilst you should buy it at a resale keep for $1 in only some months and watch it on every occasion you need. Or simply order it from Netflix. You could have your film withinside the mail in only some days!

2. The telecellsmartphone invoice changed into additionally any other big difficulty for me in addition to my net invoice. Now, of direction you may reduce those payments absolutely in case you sincerely do now no longer want them, however I ought to have them for my paintings. I went to my nearby telecellsmartphone corporation and talked to them approximately the charge. I ended up being capable of pay simply $sixty nine every month for each offerings in preference to the $a hundred thirty I changed into paying. If you don't want the net for paintings or school, it's miles first-rate to head in advance and feature it and your own home telecellsmartphone close off and use handiest your mobileular telecellsmartphone for those offerings.

3. Speaking of mobileular telephones, we are able to sincerely run up a big invoice every month. The manner I bumped off this invoice changed into at my nearby Wal-Mart. Yes you heard me right. I went to Wal-Mart, picked up a $10 pay as you go telecellsmartphone and commenced searching at plans. I do now no longer want the net on my telecellsmartphone considering that I even have it at domestic, so I am capable of pay

$35 in keeping with month for limitless speak and textual content. Now, if I wanted the net on my telecellsmartphone and did now no longer have it at domestic, I may want to pay $50 in keeping with month for limitless speak textual content and web. This is a big financial savings over any agreement you'll get with a mobileular telecellsmartphone. The telephones are simply as correct as those you get with a agreement and also you don ' t ought to be caught with a few obsolete turn telecellsmartphone. If you're seeking to keep cash to your mobileular telecellsmartphone invoice, test out the pay as you go mobileular telephones to be had to your area.

4. Consider operating from domestic. This is a big cash saver. Before I labored from domestic, I needed to pay a babysitter to observe my 3 youngsters, I needed to pay for fueloline to get backward and forward to paintings and the listing went on and on. Now my youngsters live at domestic with me whilst I paintings in my office, saving me over $1,2 hundred a month plus fueloline and so on. Figure out if it's miles viable so one can do business from home and decide how a good deal cash you'll keep in case you do.

5. Stop buying objects you need to make bills on. If you will buy a automobile, ensure you've got got the coins to do so. The remaining automobile I bought after attempting to find numerous hours on line price me $500. I bought my different automobile for $500 and paid coins for the only I very own now. The automobile isn't always beat up or a rust bucket, it's miles a ninety four Lincoln that runs like a charm. If you make an effort to look for those deals, you will keep a ton in hobby withinside the lengthy run.

6. Buy used and keep the difference. Going together with now no longer making bills on anything, forestall shopping for the whole thing emblem new. Find used objects and keep your cash. Six years in the past I bought a used washing machine and dryer. I am very choosy approximately my clothes, so after 2 hours of scrubbing them out, I changed into equipped to apply them. I paid $50 overall for each and they're presently in my laundry room doing an excellent job. Granted, I do now no longer use the dryer often, however it's miles there after I want it. You can try this with all your appliances, however you want to ensure you have become an amazing deal. For example, I went to shop for a used deep freeze. It price $one hundred, so I determined I desired to examine costs with a brand new one and determined I may want to get a bigger one which changed into on sale at a nearby shop new for $60. Don ' t anticipate simply due to the fact it's miles being

bought as used which you have become the bottom charge you may.

7. Cut up the credit score playing cards and pay them off. I individually have in no way owned a credit score card and I in no way need to. I watched my mother and father ought to document financial ruin because of overspending on credit score playing cards. If you presently very own a credit score card, reduce it up, name the corporation and spot if they'll decrease your hobby charge then begin paying them off. Once they're paid off, do now no longer observe for brand spanking new ones. Live on what coins you've got got to your pocket and do now no longer collect debt.

8. Consider quitting smoking and ingesting. The common smoker

spends over $one hundred fifty every month on cigarettes and relying on how a good deal you're ingesting you can be spending upwards of $one hundred on that as properly. That is $3,000 a 12 months that you may positioned in the direction of some thing greater important. Saving cash and being frugal has plenty to do with being healthful as properly and simply believe the quantity of cash you'll emerge as saving on destiny health practitioner payments in case you end now.

9. Shop at thrift stores and backyard sales. You might imagine that you'll now no longer discover whatever which you like in case you buy from thrift stores or backyard sales, however the fact is you may discover superb treasures. For example, my complete dwelling room is provided with Ashley furniture. I sold it at a backyard sale from an aged couple. It become thoroughly cared for and I spent a complete of $2 hundred for a couch, loveseat, and chairs. All of the pix in my domestic have come from thrift stores, in addition to all the televisions I very own. You can buy a 40-inch tv from a thrift save for approximately $40. This is due to the fact they commonly do now no longer have the far flung with them, however wager what; you may order a typical far flung from Amazon for approximately $10. So you come to be spending round $50 for the complete thing!

10. Find activities that don't fee any cash. Often instances humans become bored and that they determine that they need to head spend a few cash to entertain themselves, as a substitute discover activities which are free. Such as a hike

withinside the woods, touring your nearby park, taking your youngsters swimming withinside the river or coaching them approximately volunteering on the nearby animal shelter. You also can watch your nearby paper without cost activities which are being held on your city consisting of parades, automobile indicates or prepare dinner dinner offs.

Chapter 4

And There is More!

There are even greater approaches so as to store cash every and each day! I recognize at this factor you'll be getting a touch overwhelmed, however pick out some cash saving thoughts from this ee-e book and put in force them. Once you're capable of do them with consistency upload some greater. This isn't always all or not anything here. Remember, saving only a little will assist you come to be advocated to store even greater!

1. Take gain of give up of season sales. Did you understand that you may get logo call garments modern for actually pennies at the dollar? At the give up of every season apparel is going on sale, in case you watch the costs you may be capable of get $one hundred shirts for a pair bucks! When you've got got developing youngsters that is a splendid manner to maintain them in elegant

apparel with out breaking the bank. What I do is buy one or sizes larger than what my toddler is currently

sporting in order that the brand new garments will healthy while that season comes round again. You also can try this for vacation decorations, costumes, or even buy your Christmas gives for the following yr proper after this years Christmas! You will come to be saving approximately 90% on Christmas and you may be organized for the subsequent yr!

2. Cook all your food at domestic. If you discover that you're going out to devour greater than as soon as a month, you actually need to consider cooking greater food at domestic. You see, for what you spend on one meal at a quick meals place, you may make dinner for 4 at domestic and it's going to be plenty greater healthy.

3. If some thing is broken, do now no longer throw it away, repair it! We stay in a society wherein the entirety is disposable, however in case you actually need to store cash, discover ways to repair the matters which are broken.

4. Rent rather than very own. There are folks who will disagree with this, however in case you lease a residence rather than buy it, you don't should pay domestic proprietors insurance, you don't should fear approximately how you'll pay for a brand new water heater, simply name the owner and allow them to cope with it.

5. Move to a smaller less expensive residence. This is one which receives a whole lot of humans. We need our kids to have their very own bedrooms, to have a massive residence to stay in and we need others to assume we're nicely off. If you're deciding to buy greater residence than you actually need, you're losing your cash. I needed to recollect this after I become dwelling in a 5 bed room residence understanding we without a doubt handiest used among the rooms. So plenty area become now no longer being used, consequently a lot of my cash become being wasted. Look right into a smaller less expensive residence in case you discover that each one of your property isn't always being used.

6. Plant a garden. Gardening may be very less expensive and it may produce plenty of splendid meals so as to devour. You also can promote the extra at your nearby farmers marketplace that allows you to make a few extra money at the side!

7. Raise your very own chickens. Many humans have hassle

ingesting the chickens that they raise, so for the ones humans, simply get enough

chickens to supply the range of eggs you want every day! If you've got got more promote them. In the summer, you may permit your chickens to roam your backyard and devour up all of the insects in conjunction with a few grass to reduce on hen feed.

8. Learn the way to reduce your very own hair or at the least your youngsters's hair. In our house, I reduce everyone's hair besides my very own. I even have very lengthy hair and once I need it trimmed I am inclined to pay the $eight to have it done, however most effective a few times a 12 months. If you may reduce your very own hair this is high-quality, if now no longer discover a affordable salon and feature them do it at the cheap.

9. Dying your very own hair also can prevent a ton of cash. With salon charges sky rocketing, you may store approximately $one hundred on every occasion you dye your hair at domestic relying on how lengthy it is.

10. Take snacks with you anywhere you cross. How regularly do you bounce withinside the automobile to move someplace and the youngsters begin complaining that they're hungry? You emerge as preventing through a quick meals joint and spending $forty on junk meals. Instead, clutch a few Ziploc baggage and stuff them complete of healthful snacks. The subsequent time the youngsters say they're, hungry hand them a bag and be for your way.

Chapter 5

Final Tips for You to Save Money!

In this subsequent chapter, I am going to present you ten greater pointers that will help you store cash. Here are ten greater pointers to assist prevent cash each day!

1. Find out in case your financial institution is charging you costs. What occurs in case your financial institution account receives overdrawn through accident? How a lot do you emerge as paying? If you locate which you are paying costs at your financial institution, discover a financial institution that works for you. For example, my financial institution gives a plan without cost that lets in you to overdraw through $six hundred so long as you repay the stability inside a month. This is high-quality in case there's a few kind of emergency and also you don ' t should fear approximately paying $30 an afternoon in overdraft costs!

2. Have your payments robotically taken from your financial institution account every month. Life is speedy and every so often we neglect about to ship that invoice or bounce on-line to pay it, so rather of having charged past due costs every

    month, simply join up to vehiclemobile pay your payments every month. This can store some hundred greenbacks in past due costs every 12 months.

3. Sell the belongings you don ' t want! Don ' t provide away the garments that your youngsters have out grown, take them to a thrift save and promote them on consignment or higher but have a backyard sale and make a few more cash. I usually ship the entirety to the thrift save due to the fact I don ' t have a lot time to devise a backyard sale and that they do all of the paintings for me. You do want to apprehend they'll take a percent of what your stuff sells for though.

4. Stop shopping for paper towels (until of route you've got got a chit that makes them free). Instead of purchasing paper towels, cross purchase a % of white wash cloths for $three that you'll use

in particular for cleaning.

5. Freeze the gadgets you purchase in bulk. A few weeks in the past I went to the neighborhood cut price grocery shop and that they had Coffee Mate creamer on sale for two for a dollar. This stuff may be very expensive, so I bought numerous. I knew that if I did now no longer use them speedy they might cross bad, so rather, I positioned them withinside the freezer and every week I can clutch one out to apply. I now have sufficient creamer for numerous months and stored around $80! You can freeze lots of gadgets you locate on sale like this, and in case you don't recognise ask a person who works at the shop, they could normally inform you.

6. If you're going to run your appliances (dishwasher, washing machine, dryer) run them at night. The off height hour charges for strength are less expensive than throughout the day!

7. Save all your alternate for a 12 months. Each time you empty your wallet or your purse, positioned your free alternate in a jar, on the give up of the 12 months deposit this alteration right into a financial savings account.

8. Do you get a tax go back? Many human beings with youngsters get a tax go back every 12 months, a lot of those human beings additionally emerge as losing this cash on gadgets they do now no longer truely want. Instead of losing your tax go back, create a plan to apply it to pay up your payments for numerous months in advance, or use it to pay down a number of that debt. This is a high-quality threat with a purpose to advantage your self withinside the days to come.

9. Use a thirty-day plan. If you're in the shop and also you see some thing which you need, positioned it again at the shelf and watch for thirty days. If in thirty days you continue to need the object, see if you may suit it into your budget, however possibilities are you're going to neglect about approximately the object due to the fact you most effective desired it on impulse.

10. Need it or need it. Many humans should realise there may be a distinction among want and need. They pass into the shop see an object they need and inform themselves they want it for this precise reason. A want is some thing that you'll now no longer be capable of stay with out. A need is manifestly some

thing you could stay with out however might surely like. Ask your self in case you actually need the object earlier than shopping for it.

Chapter 6

How to Get Out of Debt for Good

Throughout this ee-e book, I actually have given you recommendations on the way to store cash, however what are you prepurported to do with the cash you're saving? Of path you could placed it withinside the financial institution in a financial savings account, however earlier than you do which you need to get your self out of debt.

It does now no longer be counted what sort of debt you've got got, the method I am going to educate you'll get you absolutely out of debt withinside the shortest quantity of time possible.

First, I need you to get a pen and paper and begin writing down all the debt you very own and what sort of you presently very own on that debt. Like this:

Medical $6,543

MasterCard $4,154

Visa $2,894

Car $7,325

And so on. Now as soon as you've got got your listing, you'll discover the debt which you owe the least quantity on. Using the above example, you'll need first of all the Visa card. If your minimal month-to-month fee is $2 hundred, I need you to price range that $2 hundred into your month-to-month payments. I additionally need you to feature an more $50 to $a hundred onto the fee relying on how lots you could afford.

Keep making your minimal bills at the relaxation of your payments till the Visa is paid in full. Next, you'll pass directly to the MasterCard. Let's say you've got got been paying $three hundred a month towards that debt, I need you to take that

$three hundred plus the $2 hundred you had been paying in your Visa in addition to the $50 to $a hundred greenbacks you introduced directly to the minimal fee and pay that every one in the direction of your MasterCard. This might make your fee $550 to $six hundred greenbacks a month.

After you've got got paid off your MasterCard, you're going to transport directly to the subsequent bill. In this case you'll start paying off your scientific payments. So, in case you are paying a minimal of $a hundred greenbacks in step with month towards your scientific payments, you'll take the $2 hundred you had been paying towards your Visa earlier than it became paid off, plus the $50 to $a hundred more you had been sending in, upload to that the $three hundred you had been paying towards your MasterCard earlier than it became paid off, and you'll be sending $650-$seven hundred greenbacks in step with month towards your scientific payments.

You will preserve this system till all your debt is paid off. Then, you'll hold following the recommendations I actually have given you on this ee-e book to make certain you do now no longer accrue greater debt. It is critical which you take the cash you had been paying towards preceding payments and price range it for the subsequent bill, due to the fact in any other case you'll discover your self spending and losing all of that cash that need to be going to payments. Once your debt is paid off, you want to set it up together along with your financial institution so the cash is deposited at once right into a financial savings account every and each month.

Doing this may make certain which you aren't losing your cash, however putting in a pleasing nest egg for your self and your family.

This system is simple, however relying on the quantity of debt, you've got got it may make the effort. Remember the top I gave you approximately your tax return, in case you do get one, you could additionally use this to pay down those money owed making the system pass lots, lots faster.

Chapter 7

Frugal Lifestyle

Living frugally and with out debt is a life-style and it could make the effort that allows you to get used to it, however it's so releasing that it's far really well worth all the paintings that is going into it. When making a decision which you need to stay frugally and with out debt, take a seat down down and make a listing of motives why you need to do so.

Keep this listing of motives nearby in order that in case you begin to sense like you're lacking out on sure matters in lifestyles you'll be reminded of what your desires are. One of the guidelines in our residence is if we don't have a chit for it, we do now no longer buy it. So, in case you surely are looking some thing seek the net for a chit for it or simply wait till it is going on sale.

Another a part of dwelling the frugal life-style is looking after the matters

you've got got and respecting what you've got got spent your cash on. So what in case you very own a
$50 couch, that is $50 from your pocket, deal with it and admire it.

Finally, I need to speak to you approximately passing at the frugal lifestyle. How extremely good wouldn't it not experience if you can say your kids might in no way be in debt? What approximately in case you knew that they might in no way cross with out or need due to the fact you taught them a way to store and spend cash wisely. If for no different motive than this, I desire which you take the guidelines on this ee-e book and put in force them into your life.

You should recognize earlier than you make a decision to make those modifications, that residing frugally and saving cash does take a few greater paintings in life! It does take giving up a few conveniences, however believe me in case you observe thru with this in some months you won 't even pass over them.

Now, how can you put in force those modifications? As I referred to earlier than, I need you to select out some of the guidelines I actually have given you and begin making the ones modifications on your life. Once you've got got carried out those modifications, after some weeks upload some extra modifications.

You don ' t need to make too many modifications immediately due to the fact in case you do you may locate that they may be tougher to paste to. Most human beings need to make big modifications of their lives and that they fail due to the fact they genuinely are asking an excessive amount of of themselves. But in case you upload in small modifications, you may slightly be aware them and

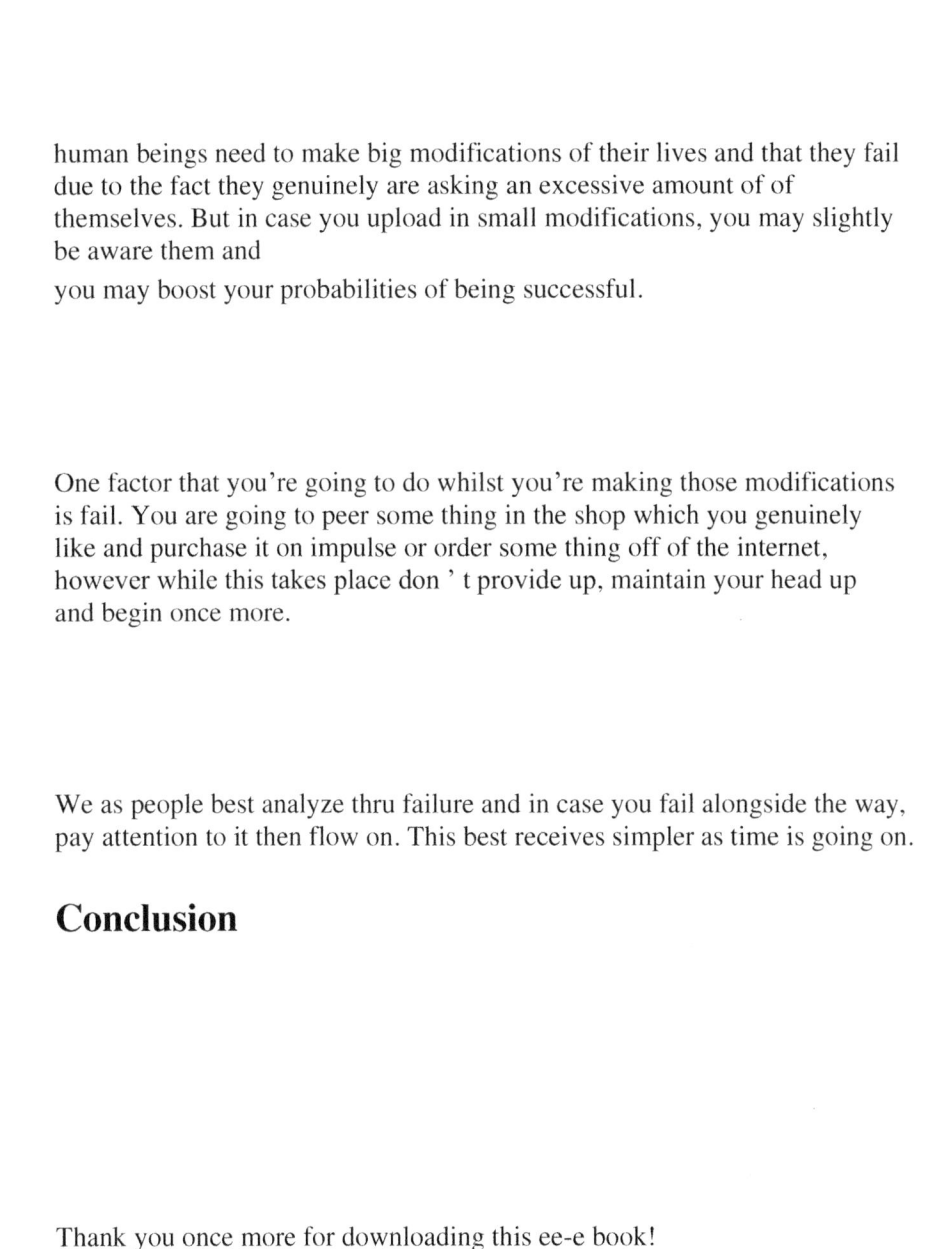

you may boost your probabilities of being successful.

One factor that you're going to do whilst you're making those modifications is fail. You are going to peer some thing in the shop which you genuinely like and purchase it on impulse or order some thing off of the internet, however while this takes place don ' t provide up, maintain your head up and begin once more.

We as people best analyze thru failure and in case you fail alongside the way, pay attention to it then flow on. This best receives simpler as time is going on.

Conclusion

Thank you once more for downloading this ee-e book!

I desire this ee-e book turned into capin a position that will help you to store cash, get out of debt and stay a extra frugal life!

The subsequent step is to get commenced the use of those guidelines and paying off that debt!

Spending Less and Loving It:

Chapter 1- The Makings of a Budget

In a Society wherein cash has little to no which means on a each day basis, human beings generally tend to spend what they need, once they need to. Why this is probably excellent on the time, on the subject of the give up of the month, human beings are regularly quick on budget and pressure so that you can make the payments happen. If best they might have notion thru their purchases previous to beginning them, they could have averted the trouble withinside the first place. So, how do human beings ensure that they've all of the cash they want so that you can now no longer pressure on the give up of a month?

The solution is referred to as a finances. Having this type of accessible equipment at your fingertips can genuinely have an impact on how and wherein you spend your cash on a each day basis. The unhappy a part of the problem is, now no longer many human beings recognize or understand a way to finances their cash so that you can reap monetary success. It's my aim that will help you recognize what makes up a finances and the way the use of you will extensively enhance your monetary scenario and coins flow.

So, let's begin at the start and examine what a finances is and a way to construct one to fit your private needs. Once you've got got a organization information of
budgeting, you may be capable of construct your personal and spot the advantages it may provoke on your life.

A finances is basically a device that suggests you wherein your cash is going and wherein your cash comes from. It then takes your profits and subtracts your fees from it, displaying you when you have cash left on the give up of the month, or in case you are going to be quick on funds. Once you've got got all your payments plugged into this finances, you may genuinely see wherein your cash is going and wherein modifications want to be made so that you can make sure which you do have cash left on the give up of the month.

Building a finances is pretty simple, and your computer's workplace files could have templates that will help you make your personal finances. These spreadsheets will calculate your findings for you, taking the guesswork out of the process. If you've got got the resource, strive plugging on your fees and profits and spot what it tells you.

One factor which you really want to maintain in thoughts while constructing a finances is the miscellaneous cash you spend which you won't even comprehend is leaving your hand. Think approximately while you prevent to seize a cup of espresso or a soda. These transactions do have an effect on your finances, despite the fact that they appear petty and small. Adding the 2 to 3 bucks you spent on the espresso save ought to have an impact on your finances in case you do it repeatedly.

So, while constructing a finances, consist of on every occasion you spend cash or take make cash. Every penny can have an effect on your normal economic state of affairs, even though it looks as if a small and unworthy transaction. If it enables, strive searching at your financial institution statements and spot wherein you used your card or withdrew cash from the ATM. These all upload up withinside the give up, and only a few bucks may want to make a large distinction while you want to pay that energy invoice on the give up of the month!

Are you prepared to construct your very own finances? Then spherical up your receipts and bills, and let's see wherein your cash is going. If it's a surprise to you, then it is able to be a outstanding time to alternate your spending behavior a good way to be capable of shop cash and spot a superb discern on the give up of the month.

In the subsequent chapters, I'm going to provide you a few hints and recommendation on approaches you may spend much less cash so you may have a superb-searching finances. I'm additionally going to get a bit innovative in a way to spend your cash and approaches you may spend much less on objects and offerings you buy on a ordinary basis. Are you prepared?

Chapter 2- Helpful Ways to Budget Money

As I referred to withinside the preceding chapter, there are numerous approaches that humans finances their cash. I use a spreadsheet on my laptop that fills withinside the blanks for me. However, there are different strategies to budgeting that could training session higher in your persona and spending behavior. In this chapter, I'm going to provide you a few approaches that humans finances their cash that enables them to shop and nevertheless experience like they have got their economic state of affairs beneathneath control.

Cash Envelopes

Some humans locate that they spend much less once they have coins handy as opposed to the use of a credit score or a debit card. Try setting cash in an envelope earlier than going out and most effective permit your self to spend what's in that envelope. Once it's far gone, you can't spend any extra. This will assist you to now no longer overspend simply due to the fact you've got got the cash in an account.

Separate Bank Accounts

In an afternoon and age wherein getting a financial institution account is nearly free, strive splitting your cash into bills which can be targeted for that cause will assist you to position your cash wherein it belongs because it comes in. Many on-line webweb sites let you nickname your bills, so having those bills may be an smooth manner to position your cash wherein it wishes to be and remove the temptation of spending it proper away.

Writing it down because it Happens

Even aleven though many humans don ' t stability a checkbook anymore, it's far nevertheless an excellent practice. You won't even use checks, however convey round a checkbook check in and file on every occasion you spend cash. This will provide you with a clean view of while and the way your cash is being spent. Once you recognize wherein your cash is going, you'll be capable of alternate how it ' s spent.

Rounding Up

This is one in every of my favored approaches to shop a bit more cash. Every time that I use my debit card, I will spherical the full up the following greenback. When I reconcile my assertion on the give up of the month, the cash that I rounded up is placed right into a financial savings account that I actually have for vacations. This is a painless manner to shop cash due to the fact it's essentially saving much less than a greenback a transaction!

Change to the Piggy Bank

This idea follows the equal concept as the only with the debit card. With coins, as opposed to diving for that penny, permit the alternate to accumulate. When you arrive home, however that alternate withinside the piggy financial institution and permit it to accumulate for a while. After your field is full, take it to a Coin big name or financial institution and feature them matter it for you! You can be amazed how tons you may shop with setting your alternate in a piggy financial institution!

Computer Programs

If you've got got a laptop, you may extra than probable have software program that you may
generate a finances spreadsheet on. Use your sources and provide your self a visible illustration of what your finances looks as if and locate locations wherein you may alternate it a good way to see higher results.

Budgeting isn't always sitting down with a bit of paper and balancing each cent. It may be withinside the manner which you have a take a observe spending, the way you shop your cash earlier than it's spent, and the way you manage the excess or deficit. Many humans get harassed out while the concept of budgeting comes into play due to the fact they experience that it is going to be like an novice accounting job. Don't consider it in that manner. Think approximately it as a manner to recognize wherein your cash is going and why your budget appear to be they do when you attain the give up of the month.

Once you convert your perspectives on budgeting, it'll be a miles less complicated task. You may even locate that locating approaches to spend much less and keep cash may be fun! Money shouldn't should be stressful, despite the fact that it's essential to survive.

Chapter 3- Creative Ways to Save Money

It can be difficult to keep cash, particularly whilst you sense such as you won't have some thing left after you pay all of the bills. However, in case you test the small matters you could do to spend much less, you may locate that you could keep cash for a wet day. Saving cash isn't clean, however it's miles feasible in case you exercise willpower and understand that the cash you're saving will serve an awesome purpose.

For a few, having a standard financial savings account isn't sufficient. If the cash is there, it's clean to spend. While this is probably the maximum traditional and simplest manner to keep cash, it's also the less complicated manner to get admission to your stored cash and use it up earlier than you realise it. Let's test a few approaches you could creatively positioned cash apart so you don't spend it earlier than you reap your financial savings goals.

Make a Contest to See How Much You Can Save on a Specific Item

If you're a aggressive man or woman, you may revel in this suggestion. Even in case you're competing towards yourself, you could nonetheless make this give you the results you want. Try to locate deals on gadgets which you purchase and use on a ordinary basis. The much less steeply-priced you could locate it, the extra factors you earn. Take away the sale charge from the everyday retail charge and spot how an awful lot you stored. The extra you keep, the higher. I love doing this as a family. I store at one grocery save and my husband will visit any other. As we store, we are able to see which save has the higher charge on which products. The man or woman who can locate the maximum financial savings is the winner.

Finding as Many Coupons as Possible

Coupons are a great manner to keep cash instantly. By taking the time to locate store and producer coupons, you can be saving on an object this is already discounted. Clipping and locating coupons may be a time eating venture, however the cash that it saves may be astounding. You don't should be an intense couponer if you want to make coupons give you the results you want and prevent a number of cash. Just use what you could locate whilst you locate them. On average, I have a tendency to keep 100 bucks every grocery purchasing ride due to the fact I can locate coupons and in save specials that upload as much as excellent financial savings.

Savings Jar with a Savings Thermometer

You will see this technique whilst humans are saving in colleges or in jobs for the gain of a fundraiser. Why now no longer make your financial savings a fundraiser inside itself? Set up a jar that you could positioned more money and alternate in. After including your cash, fill withinside the thermometer to mirror how an awful lot is in that jar. For example, in case you ' re saving for a vacation, you could have an stop aim in your thermometer with a purpose to inform you which you have stored sufficient cash to fulfill the expenses. This may be an interesting manner for anybody to peer how properly your financial savings is coming alongside and get them excited for the stop aim.

Have a Piggy Bank Competition

Kids love this. It allows them to discover ways to keep. Give every of your kids a piggy financial institution that they may be accountable for setting cash in. Have a time body and make certain that the kid can not see into the piggy financial institution. After the term has elapsed, empty the banks and spot who has stored the maximum cash. You can then take the cash stored and positioned it right into a financial savings account on the financial institution and allow it live there.

Find Savings in Unusual Places

You can be amazed at a number of the locations that financial savings will display itself. By going on-line earlier than you store or buy services, you is probably capable of locate financial savings in a few difficult to understand locations. It will make the effort and research in your component to locate the financial savings and make certain they may be legitimate, however you extra than in all likelihood will stand to locate some thing that you could use!

Learning Where to Save

Even aleven though stores promote the identical product does now no longer imply that they've the identical prices. For example, grocery shops have reputations for being the " steeply-priced " save or the " cheap " save. After purchasing at some shops, locate which save generally gives you the high-quality offers and store there. Even aleven though any other save may have a higher charge on one object doesn ' t imply that purchasing there'll prevent cash withinside the lengthy run. You ' re searching out an area with a purpose to always provide you decrease prices, despite the fact that you could pay extra for simply one object.

Treasure Stashes

When I changed into a child, my mom had a dependancy of stashing cash away withinside the residence for a wet day. She known as them her treasure stashes due to the fact she now and again amazed herself whilst she got here throughout the cash. It were so nicely hidden that she forgot that she had even positioned it there! This will be a terrific manner to store in case you are barely forgetful and feature more money to store. It also can be amusing to locate stashes which you have forgotten existed!

Listing the Pros and Cons Prior to Purchase

For foremost purchases, make the effort and listing the advantageous and poor elements of the buy. Do you actually need it? Can you locate it at a higher fee? Will every other logo accomplish the identical dreams for much less? By reading your buy earlier than you are making it, you'll both discover how proper of an concept it's miles, or you'll discover if you may stay with out it. Just taking the time to reflect onconsideration on it may prevent the cash!

Finding innovative methods to store cash may be each amusing and rewarding. Also, making saving a own circle of relatives task receives absolutely each person worried and teaches your kids the fee of saving for the future. It may take some time so that you can store the quantity of cash you want to store, however it's going to upload up through the years and you'll be capable of see the blessings withinside the future. Spending much less and saving greater may be amusing and train you and your own circle of relatives the fee of a dollar.

Chapter 4- Learning to Investigate Purchases

With as a lot opposition as there's obtainable for locations to promote their merchandise, a person can have a decrease fee than the primary region you switch to. While searching at your object on line and in shops may be time consuming, saving extra cash might be really well worth it withinside the end. Stores take gain of the truth that it's handy simply to shop for what they ought to provide. They don't do not forget that the competitor can be imparting a miles higher fee for the identical object.

By taking the time to investigate and look into capability purchases on line and in keep, you're getting ready your self to get the first-class fee. You can also be exposing your self to offers and specials that won't be obvious withinside the advertisements which might be published withinside the newspaper and on line. Just a touch more time can prevent an entire lot of extra cash!

Cell Phone Apps

With the arrival of smartphones, there had been lots of brilliant apps that let you store. If you may't make it to a pc to do your contrast purchasing, pull up your app keep and discover a few particularly rated apps that let you to make an knowledgeable decision. You can locate apps approximately wherein to locate the most inexpensive gas, the most inexpensive tickets, or some thing else you want to buy. In some moments, you cellphone can prevent a bundle. Thank you, cellphone!

Comparison Websites

There are a ton of web sites obtainable with a view to provide you with the costs of various locations promoting what you're looking to shop for. These have lately come to be famous for airline tickets and travel, however you may locate them for nearly some thing which you are purchasing for. Take the time and notice who's promoting what you need for the first-class fee and pass from there. Just due to the fact it's handy doesn't intended that it's miles the first-class buy for you. Do your research!

Price Match Guarantees

A lot of shops need your business, and they may provide you a fee in shape assure if you may show that every other store is promoting the identical object for a less expensive fee. However, you need to be cautious with a number of those policies. Some locations won't honor costs which might be contingent upon a shopper's card. However, in case you discover a sale fee that you're feeling you may fee in shape, it doesn't harm to try!

Online Prices

When purchasing, the store's on line fee is regularly much less than what you should buy it for withinside the keep. Also, there is probably an internet sale for that object that isn't venerated withinside the keep. If you want on the spotaneous gratification, then recover from it. If it's less expensive on line, watch for it to be shipped and buy it there. This, of course, is going for an object that isn't wanted immediately.

Checking for Sales

Stores extrade their income periodically. Some can also additionally extrade them weekly or biweekly. Figure out the income of the shops which you keep and whilst they're because of extrade. When the brand new income come out, test up on them proper away and notice if you may locate a few proper financial savings that you may inventory up on.

Stocking up on merchandise whilst they're on sale is a first rate manner to store cash, granted that the objects aren't perishable.

Buy Used if Possible

When it involves a few objects, you is probably capable of discover what you're seeking out at a thrift shop and keep your self a variety of cash. Buying used garb and different items isn't shameful, however smart. People are continuously upgrading and casting off the old, so via way of means of taking gain of this, you may discover objects which can be almost new at a fragment of the cost!

Wait if Necessary

Things will subsequently move on sale. If you discover which you need to buy some thing however it's far too expensive, wait it out a touch while. Either the shop will mark down the fee, or the fee will drop on its own. Even in case you don't get what you need while it's extraordinarily popular, you may nonetheless experience the advantages of it at a later date!

Call Ahead to Confirm

When shops have sales, the objects every so often promote out quickly, specifically while they may be on the stop of the sale. Don't waste a while via way of means of going to the shop to buy those objects with out calling and checking their availability earlier than you go away home. It may be a wasted experience in case you display as much as discover that they bought out of what you meant to buy days earlier than. All shops have a manner you may touch them, so don't be afraid to utilize this resource.

The aim to having a notable price range and spending much less is understanding a way to paintings the system. People are so set on being immediately gratified via way of means of purchases that they frequently spend a lot greater than they could in the event that they had been to attend only some days. Don't be that form of person. Allow your self to be affected person and look forward to the fine possibility to buy. Your price range and your pockets may be smiling at you later on!

Chapter 5- The Trick to Finding a Creative Budget

Spending much less cash is simply one manner to get your price range to have a fantastic determine on the stop of the month. Knowing what you may spend and tracking the way you spend your cash can surely assist you notice what your spending conduct are and the way they may be modified so that it will make sure which you are saving in preference to spending. If a conventional price range simply isn't reducing it for you, then there are different approaches to price range your cash and nonetheless attain the equal advantages of a conventional price range.

You can also additionally have visible seminars accomplished on approaches to price range which have stored human beings cash via way of means of wondering outdoor the standard spending conduct that we're used to today. In this chapter, I need to test a number of those innovative budgeting techniques and the way they will let you to keep your difficult earned cash for what you really need to spend it on. I additionally need to feature multiple different thoughts to help you get into the saving mindset.

Money Envelope Method

This approach has been extraordinarily a hit for plenty human beings. The idea is which you use coins for everything. Having the coins in hand, you divide the cash into precise envelopes which can be committed to positive bills. For example, you may have an envelope to your rent, the automobile payment, groceries, or anything else you've got got that could be a normal expense. You are confined to the cash in that envelope. If you run out of grocery cash, then you definitely ought to wait till the following spherical of budgeting comes around. The envelope approach has taught human beings the significance of looking what they spend and spending their cash a touch greater wisely.

Money Jars

Money jars observe alongside the equal idea, besides they may be used for saving. Set up for jars, one for vacation, one for outings, one for extras, and anything else you may use more money for. Put the spare coins and cash out of your cash envelopes into those jars and permit the cash to accumulate. You aren't handiest the use of a notable manner to tune your spending, you also are saving for some thing that you may have a laugh doing!

Daily Savings Method

I even have visible this proposal across the vacations with reference to having present cash. What takes place is, you keep a dollar (or anything denomination you need) the primary day, bucks the second one day, and so forth, doubling the quantity each day or weekly. This cash is then placed into financial savings to fund anything you desire to apply it for. The concept is that via way of means of the stop of a time period, your cash has extensively accelerated and you've stored greater than you may via way of means of different techniques.

Budget Box

A price range field is a manner this is much like cash envelopes. With the field, you keep every receipt and every invoice you paid and it's far filed beneathneath its customized category. At the stop of the month, you may pull out your receipts and examine what you spent your cash on and where. This is a superb manner to capture useless spending/

Monthly Savings Plan

Having a hard and fast quantity which you placed into your financial savings account on a monthly

foundation will assist you to mentally component with that cash earlier than it ' s even for your hands. I like to position a positive percent of my paycheck into my financial savings account and paintings with the relaxation of it once I price range. By taking this cash out first, I am now no longer making plans on the use of it, and the price range might be focused at the relaxation of the paycheck.

Meals at the Cheap

This is a a laugh approach that I got here throughout on line and feature simply began out to apply recently. What you do is, you pass grocery purchasing and purchase your meat and veggies in bulk. These meats and veggies want on the way to be frozen due to the fact you will shop an amazing part of what you purchase withinside the freezer. Once you've got got located your meat and veggies at a bargain, you'll put together it in bulk for numerous meals. For example, you'll have sufficient taco meat that you may make tacos and nachos for 2 exceptional meals. By getting ready your meals at as soon as, you store your self each time and cash.

Teaching Children to Save

Since we stay in a time in which financial savings isn't always emphasized, coaching your kids a way to store younger will put together them to store as adults. When they
are vintage sufficient to apprehend what saving is, take them and deliver them their very own financial savings account on the financial institution. Then once they have greater cash, take them to the financial institution with you and allow them to deposit it. This will train them now no longer most effective approximately saving, however it's going to train them a way to financial institution.

Eliminating Unnecessary Spending

We all have a vice that we spend cash unnecessarily on. Coffee is mine. I realize I even have used it for instance some instances on this book. I love espresso. Not simply any espresso, However fancy espresso which you purchase at espresso shops. However, this espresso is expensive. In order to take away that pointless expense, I even have discovered to locate creamers and different components to make my espresso fancy at home. This saves me cash daily, and I can get nearly the identical outcomes as my barista did.

Learning exceptional strategies to saving and budgeting may be noticeably helpful, specifically when you have a totally constrained income. Having an amazing idea of what you're spending and the way you may store will assist you to construct an amazing attitude on what cash is and in which it is going for your life.

Chapter 6- Looking Forward to the Future

Our society has end up certainly considered one among spenders in place of savers. We haven't visible the actual outcomes of this modification yet, However as soon as we start to get older, our era goes to battle to live on. This will be because of the truth that retirement and our futures appear to date away that we might alternatively stay withinside the second now. However, in case you take time to consider in which you may be while you hit retirement age, you could now no longer just like the image this is provided to you.

Saving is an essential factor in making sure that we are able to live on as soon as we hit retirement age. Learning a way to store now whilst our society is telling us to spend can truly have an effect on your destiny as a senior citizen. Just consider this as I provide you with a few approaches on how saving now can massively have an effect on your retirement.

401K Plans

Many employers provide 401K plans that assist their personnel to position a component in their cash into the inventory marketplace and assist them store for retirement. This is actually a deduction out of your paycheck, and it's far placed into an account to be able to take a seat down there for years. When you go away a job, in case your 401K isn't massive sufficient, they'll disperse it to you or provide you with the choice to roll it over into your new employer's plan. It is advocated which you roll it over so you don't go through the tax consequences and you may retain to store on your retirement.

IRAs

Alongside 401K's, employers may additionally provide you an IRA (Individual Retirement Account). These bills store a part of your cash for retirement and are stored at a financial institution, so they're insured like every other account. Again, in case you go away your employer, relying at the kind of IRA, you'll be pressured to roll it over or coins it out. Also, you as an person can installation your very own non-public IRA and make contributions to it. This lets in you to constantly store.

Investments

Aside from the use of company retirement resources, you may pick to make investments your cash to your own. There are some of unique styles of investments you may make to help you to develop your cash for retirement. While a few are risky, others are strong and will let you to advantage a very good increase. There are alternatives including the inventory marketplace or valuable metals. You can discover an funding so as to experience snug for you and make it paintings in your retirement financial savings.

Bonds

Bonds are some other superb manner to make investments. It is basically the authorities borrowing cash from you. You should wait a very good time period earlier than your bond is matured, however as soon as it is, you may make a earnings off of the preliminary buy price. Depending on while you buy your bonds, the hobby costs is probably bad or good. Either manner, the authorities pays you hobby for the mortgage which you are giving them!

College Savings Plan

For more youthful individuals who are making plans on going to university and organising a

career, having a university financial savings plan will assist them to set themselves up for the destiny. The behavior that they use to shop for university may be transferred afterward in existence to assist them to apprehend the significance of saving and the way it may gain then for existence. The more youthful that a person is taught to shop, the greater ingrained it turns into into how they cope with their finances.

Retirement Calculators

If you're an extended methods farfar from being capable of retire, then it is probably for your gain to have a take a observe a calculator of what professionals trust might be your important prices while you are prepared to retire. No you may inform you with 100% truth what the sector will appear to be in ten or twenty years, however they could expect what it is going to be like. By taking this statistics and making plans ahead, you stand a higher risk of saving sufficient cash so you can effortlessly retire and now no longer be required to paintings after retirement age. Also, we should have a take a observe the reality that we might not gain from social safety like retirees nowadays do. Take this into consideration while you installation a financial savings plan in your person retirement.

Focusing to your destiny will let you while the time involves retire, visit university, or maybe cross on a own circle of relatives vacation. Just due to the fact you've got got cash now does now no longer imply that you may have that cash withinside the destiny. Be clever in the way you spend and reflect onconsideration on how your spending behavior can effect your destiny in effective of bad methods. Knowing your behavior and your spending developments will assist you to expect what your finances may appear to be withinside the destiny.

Don't be unprepared for what's to come. Take the time now to awareness on saving and ensuring which you have sufficient in your destiny plans. You might be thankful which you made those adjustments now, and you'll be spending much less now and loving it!

Chapter 7- Spending Less, Saving More

It can also additionally appear stupid to assume that growing a finances ought to shop your existence. I'm now no longer speaking like a existence-saving medicine, however it can shop your way of life and your destiny plans. Once you begin to reflect onconsideration on how saving can sincerely have an effect on the way you live, what you may have withinside the destiny, and making your goals come true, you may assume two times earlier than buying that subsequent espresso on the espresso shop.

The gift sincerely does have an effect on the destiny. What you do now together along with your profits and the way you shop it's going to in the long run have an effect on your consolation tiers while you retire, or maybe if you may have the cappotential to retire. It has turn out to be manner too not unusualplace for senior residents to preserve to paintings due to the fact their social safety assessments don't cowl all in their prices. Don't you need with a purpose to experience your retirement? That is simply one purpose to reflect onconsideration on your spending and your financial savings proper now, if you have the cappotential to alternate your spending behavior.

Now which you recognise methods to finances and shop your cash, you're prepared to
make the important adjustments to make sure which you have the form of destiny which you want to live. Think approximately it as saving your existence. In essence, you're saving your destiny from being one in every of poverty and now no longer having sufficient to help your self as soon as you make a decision to retire.

Keep the guidelines that I actually have offered on this ee-e book in thoughts the following time which you get equipped to swipe a card on an impulse purchase. Will that impulse purchase make it so you are one much less meal to your older years? It is probably loopy to consider it on this respect, however understanding that it is able to imply the distinction of meals at the desk as a senior citizen can also additionally alternate your thoughts and affect you to place that buy back.

Once I found out how saving cash actually ought to have an effect on my lifestyles, I am satisfied to make the small or even the large adjustments withinside the manner that I finances and keep my cash. I understand that after I am of retirement age, I will virtually get to retire. However, I actually needed to begin that financial savings plan as a younger adult. It might be years earlier than I can retire, however understanding that I won't should rely on a person to attend to my monetary wishes makes me love spending much less and saving.

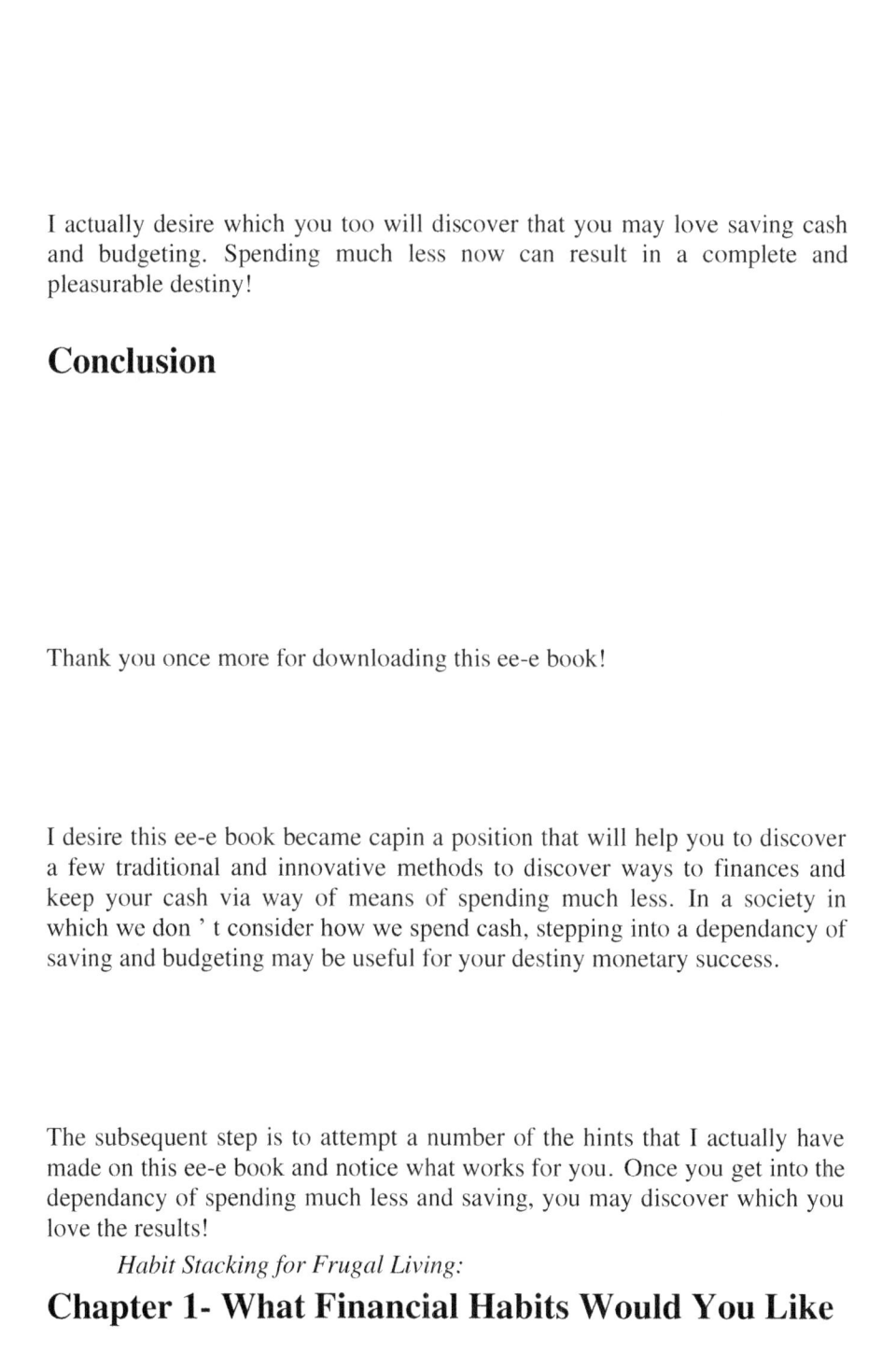

I actually desire which you too will discover that you may love saving cash and budgeting. Spending much less now can result in a complete and pleasurable destiny!

Conclusion

Thank you once more for downloading this ee-e book!

I desire this ee-e book became capin a position that will help you to discover a few traditional and innovative methods to discover ways to finances and keep your cash via way of means of spending much less. In a society in which we don't consider how we spend cash, stepping into a dependancy of saving and budgeting may be useful for your destiny monetary success.

The subsequent step is to attempt a number of the hints that I actually have made on this ee-e book and notice what works for you. Once you get into the dependancy of spending much less and saving, you may discover which you love the results!

Habit Stacking for Frugal Living:
Chapter 1- What Financial Habits Would You Like

to Change?

It's come to the cease of the month and you're combing thru your take a look at ee-e book and looking to determine out how you're going to pay that one bill. You're bored with being annoyed whilst confronted with this predicament every month. Is there any manner that you may simply be capable of pay for the whole lot and feature a few cash left over?

Many people cope with this situation. It feels just like the payments pile up and that there's constantly that one or which you don't have sufficient cash to pay. It's irritating and we'd deliver something on the way to have a few extra cash to experience ourselves with.

What if I instructed you that there has been a manner to make that happen? I'm now no longer suggesting a drastic profession alternate or something like that. However, via way of means of converting the manner we view and spend cash can assist us make our difficult earned cash move in addition every month. If you doubt what I'm pronouncing, I task you to attempt to put in force a number of those behavior into your lifestyles and notice if they'll paintings for you.

Money is a demanding and irritating detail for many. It constantly feels as aleven though you figure and by no means have something to reveal for it. Some take this because the manner it has to be, even as others need to discover methods to alternate this reality. By analyzing this ee-e book, you're pronouncing which you need to alternate this and give the opportunity to have greater on the cease of the month. You need to discover methods to alternate to be able to make this happen.

If you're equipped to alternate your monetary behavior to be able to construct monetary balance and freedom, then study in addition. You by myself should be inclined to make adjustments and paintings them into your lifestyles. Take that lead and make a few adjustments!

Chapter 2- How to Build Healthy and Lasting Habits

Habits are tough to construct, or even greater tough to dispose of whilst essential. A dependancy takes approximately thirty days to create. This method which you do the identical factor for that thirty days till it will become herbal to you. Building behavior takes motivation and observe thru. If you need to construct behavior, then you definitely have to be organized to place quite a few difficult paintings and attempt into making it happen.

The idea of dependancy stacking makes constructing behavior simpler and greater manageable. If you're taking on too many behavior at once, then you definitely 're putting your self up for failure. So, it's far endorsed which you begin with the maximum essential behavior and construct upon them to be able to make durable and powerful behavior.

Recognizing Areas that want to be Changed

In order to discover behavior which you would really like to interrupt or construct, you really want to understand what regions of your lifestyles want to be changed. In this ee-e book, we're specializing in monetary behavior, however a dependancy may be something which you do on a ordinary foundation which could have an effect on your lifestyles. Take a while and listing a number of the behavior which can be affecting your lifestyles. These may be suitable or bad. If you discover a few behavior which you would really like to put in force, spotlight the ones and discover methods to cause them to part of your lifestyles.

However, you can not extrade your whole life at once. Not simplest is that this impossible, however you ' re placing manner an excessive amount of strain on your self. With that a whole lot strain, you'll move lower back in your antique methods, in the end failing at your preliminary intentions. Take extrade in small doses. This may be completed via way of means of the use of a technique known as addiction stacking.

Habit Stacking

So, what's addiction stacking? Well, it ' s a idea utilized by a few to construct new
behavior upon current ones. For example, you need to lose weight. The first addiction that making a decision to construct goes to be enhancing your weight-reduction plan in order that it's miles healthier. After you've got got an awesome ingesting addiction, you then definately need to construct upon that addiction with exercise. Maybe after that, you selected to sign up for a

gym. These are all behavior, however behavior which have been introduced to every different gradually. If you had been to take all of them on at once, you is probably crushed and surrender earlier than you even get a risk to start.

Building a addiction begins offevolved with simple components. First of all, you need to perceive the addiction and wherein you need it to take you. Once you've got got recognized the addiction which you need to construct, you then definately need to determine what the quit end result will appearance like. Secondly, you'll need to consider the stairs that you'll want to take so as to increase this addiction into your non-public life. These steps is probably extraordinary for you than for every body else. It's incredible to take suggestions, however recognise which you are extraordinary from others and must make the stairs replicate your needs.

After you've got got recognized the behavior and the stairs which you want to take to attain the very last outcome, it's time to set desires to make the addiction a reality. Setting desires is a incredible manner to place deadlines on effects and tune your development in the direction of the quit intention. However, placing available desires may be tough inside itself.

Setting a Good Goal

When you place a intention, you need to make certain that it's miles challenging, however you're nonetheless capable of attain it. Setting a intention this is too tough to gain will simplest discourage you and make you surrender on what you need to accomplish. So, take an awesome study what you need to gain and set a intention this is available. Once you've got got a intention that meets this criteria, supply your self a term and then you'll take a look at in and display your development.

Once you've got got carried out your intention, make a brand new intention with the intention to task you again. The component approximately desires is which you want which will accomplish them and flow directly to new desires. Don't set your self lower back via way of means of attaining and intention and settling for it.

Now which you have an awesome concept of what addiction stacking and intention placing entails, let's study a few behavior you could start constructing so as to gain economic freedom and normal happiness.

Chapter 3- New Habits for Saving Money

It is probably tough which will shop cash in case you experience like any of your earnings is going to paying payments and different necessities. When shopping, you appearance with disdain on the girls who're juggling their coupons on the checkout. Saving cash is a idea that you could simplest dream approximately. However, it could be a real possibility. Let's check a few methods you could shop cash and be capable of set up a financial savings account.

Clipping Coupons

I get it. You don't need to be the demanding coupon girl on the checkout stand. You recognise the one. Watching the display to make certain the coupon tactics effectively and arguing with the cashier whilst it doesn't. Meanwhile, a line a mile lengthy builds up in the back of her.

I'm now no longer suggesting which you dumpster dive for coupons and watch the minute information of the transaction. However, coupons do have incredible benefits. If you discover a coupon for an object that you're going to buy anyway, why now no longer use it? It can prevent a whole lot of cash withinside the lengthy run. The incredible a part of coupons is that they're turning into electronic, so that you don't must spend hours looking and clipping them. You simply take a look at those you need to use.

Be cautious with coupons though. I locate that I will in reality spend extra if I discover a coupon I need to use. Only use a chit in case you're making plans on shopping the object withinside the first place.

Go on Sale Days

Sale days may be one of the maximum crowded and irritating days to go to a retail establishment. People are elbowing and combating for the gadgets at the shelves. However, if shopped proper, sale days can yield first rate financial savings. If you're grocery purchasing, income generally tend to span a time frame, so that you can go to the shop whilst it's maximum handy for you. Stores have sale advertisements that pop out on a normal basis, so with the aid of using understanding in which the gadgets you're purchasing for
are on sale, you're putting your self up for greater financial savings.

Look for Gas Stations with Lower Prices

I locate it top notch that I can force much less than a mile and locate fueloline costs that adjust approximately twenty cents in keeping with gallon. If I could have waited some greater minutes, I may want to have stored greater cash. You can. There are apps in your telephone with a view to listing the fueloline costs of nearby fueloline stations. By going to one which has a decrease in keeping with gallon fee, the cents will upload as much as a first rate quantity of financial savings over time.

Make Your Own Cleaners

Household cleaners are a quick manner to spend lots of cash in a single purchasing trip. There is one for the whole lot! However, selfmade cleaners and detergents can accomplish the identical desires as what you notice at the shelf. Sure, they take time to make, however when you have them prepared for use, you could keep a ton of cash with the aid of using now no longer shopping for a specialised product at the shop.

Don't Buy it Unless It's on Sale

If you've got got an object that you could stay with out and also you locate that it's now no longer on sale in which you're purchasing, don't purchase it till it's miles on sale or you've got got a coupon. Sometimes you can not keep away from paying complete fee for products, however if you could, attempt to keep away from shopping for it till it's miles on sale. By doing this, you could keep cash over time.

Be Able to Negotiate

There are locations that you could negotiate for a higher fee on gadgets. The vehicle dealership being one. Don't be afraid to barter for a higher fee. The shop clerk is attempting to get as lots cash out of you as possible, and that could make it intimidating and tough to shave cash off of the fee. However, you're looking to keep cash, so that you have an schedule too. Don't be afraid to talk up.

Set Up a Savings Account

Saving cash may be tough, specially whilst you don ' t have cash to keep. What I love to do is finances a small amount of cash in keeping with month to position right into a financial savings account that I do now no longer use except it ' s an emergency. Having those price range prepared and to be had can ease pressure whilst you don ' t have sufficient cash for what wishes to be paid.

Put Your Change in a Jar

I ' ve gotten to the factor in which I pay for the whole lot the usage of coins. By simplest having a sure sum of money to be had for sure elements of my price range. When that cash is gone, which means that I pass with out till the subsequent payday. Using coins, there may be continually alternate involved. So, every time I actually have alternate, I make it a dependancy to throw it right into a bucket that I coins in each so often. This is a first rate manner to keep amusing cash and now no longer have it have an effect on my price range!

Budget Your Income

One key to handling your price range is understanding in which you spend your cash. This can take a few time, however take a seat down down and determine out in which your cash goes. What payments do you want to pay and what sort of are they? How lots cash goes closer to nonsense? By understanding in which your cash goes, you may be higher capable of regulate what you ' re spending cash on and being capable of keep cash which you ' re basically throwing away.

Buy Only What is Needed

It ' s difficult whilst you see true income even as on foot via a store. However, take a second and ask your self in case you really want that object. I locate that maximum of the first rate income I locate turn out to be driven to the returned of the cabinet and turn out to be being wasted cash. So, the subsequent time you ' re searching at a first rate sale, take a second and certainly ask your self whether or not or now no longer you will truly use it or whether or not it simply seems first rate proper now.

Repurposing Old Items

If you've got got antique gadgets across the residence that may be used for exceptional purposes, then convert them! Some gadgets we haven't any use for of their supposed capacity, however in case you're creative, you could make an object feature in lots of exceptional ways. Not simplest will this maintain your house from being cluttered with gadgets which you can not use, however it's going to additionally prevent cash due to the fact you don't ought to locate an object for that purpose!

Pick Up a Side Job

For some, that is a complete impossibility. However, for others, having a small facet process that earns a bit more money can assist with the payments and having more money on the cease of the month. For example, you could babysit for a chum one night time per week or make crafts that you could sell. A facet process doesn't suggest that you need to visit a process and paintings more hours, however which you're doing some thing that could earn you more money.

Live Where You can Afford

Again, you need to recognition on necessity So as stay inside your means. So, whilst you're searching at houses which are above your means, you're putting your self up for debt. Make certain which you are locating a domestic wherein you could without problems have enough money the month-to-month bills. It may not appear like your best, however matters can extrade so you can pursue that best withinside the future.

Avoid Unnecessary Spending

People are withinside the addiction of spending cash that they don't always have. This can each be dangerous financially and in different components of your life. If you don't want Some thing, then it normally is going to waste. And if you want to preserve onto matters, it is able to without problems end up litter for your domestic.   So, ensure which you want the object earlier than you placed your cash into it.

Make a List, Stick to it
When you're going looking for groceries, make a listing and keep on with it

closely. This can take time and be irritating at first, however if you ' re most effective shopping for what you want, then you ' re now no longer shopping for in excess. Pretty soon, you may be capable of see which you ' re saving cash with the aid of using now no longer shopping for objects impulsively.

Telling your self " no " may be tough at times, in particular if you want that allows you to exit and purchase some thing you need every time you need. Don ' t restriction your self, however don ' t smash your self either. Make certain which you have an amazing stability among what you ' re incomes and what you ' re spending.

Chapter 4- New Habits for Reducing Your Debt

Debt is a not unusualplace block to monetary freedom. We stay in a time and a rustic wherein all of us loves to stay past their means. Credit card groups feed on this. You locate your self with a loan for a domestic which you virtually can not have enough money. You borrow cash from pals and own circle of relatives so that it will pay payments. There are many varieties of debt that you could fall into. How you address your debt will make a distinction in casting off it or drowning in in.

Pay More than the Minimum Payment

If you ' re capable of do it, pay greater on a invoice than you're billed. This is in particular real for credit score playing cards wherein the minimal fee regularly covers most effective a small part of the complete invoice. If you pay simply the minimal, then the hobby maintains constructing up so you ' re spending a great deal greater than you at the beginning deliberate on. Put a bit greater than the minimal fee closer to the invoice and you may keep away from quite a few this hobby.

Cut Up Your Credit Cards

This is probably tough for you, However credit score playing cards are a big supply of debt. By slicing up all however one credit score card, you're pronouncing which you are making plans on paying them off and in no way the usage of them again. I propose preserving one card available for emergencies and displaying which you are the usage of credit score. However, more than one credit score playing cards can without problems lead you to monetary ruin.

Focus on One Debt at a Time

Take a while and listing all your debts. If they encompass credit score playing cards, notice the proportion which you pay in hobby. If you've got got excessive hobby credit score playing cards, recognition on paying the ones off first. Getting rid of the playing cards with the very best hobby costs will prevent greater cash. While you recognition on paying the better hobby credit score playing cards off first, ensure that you ' re at the least making minimal bills on the opposite payments. Late costs and accruing hobby can upload as much as large trouble.

Pay Attention to Due Dates

Credit card groups like to hit you up with past due costs. Even in case your invoice indicates no past due fee, you may locate that having past due bills may be dangerous in your credit score. So, if you ' re searching to shop for a domestic or a vehicle, past due bills may be a big roadblock to this happening. Keep tune of whilst the invoice is due and make each attempt to have it mailed out or paid electronically earlier than the due date. A lot of groups provide computerized bills, so if you could preserve tune of what ' s popping out of your financial institution account, this is probably a handy course to make certain well timed fee.

Limit the Number of Debts You Have

If you ' re already in debt, you is probably guffawing at this one. However, in case you consider it, you have been the only who were given your self into debt. If you hadn ' t bought such and such on that credit score card, you then definately wouldn ' t have had the debt. So, whilst any other possibility to accrue debt comes along, assume tough and lengthy earlier than leaping into it. Some money owed are unavoidable, together with scientific payments and domestic repairs. Know the distinction among a preference debt and a essential debt.

Live Within Your Means

If you've got got a activity at a quick meals restaurant, probabilities are which you won ' t have the approach to shop for a domestic or a brand new car. Taking out loans will most effective positioned your similarly into debt. So, whilst thinking about what you want to buy and what you need to buy, examine the numbers. If you didn ' t have a loan, could you sincerely be capable of pay for it? If the solution is " no, " you then definately aren't dwelling inside your approach.

Learn to Say No to New Debt

I talked a touch approximately this above. When a brand new provide for a credit score card or keep

credit score card appears to be knocking at your door, recognize whilst to mention no. Credit card groups love your commercial enterprise due to the fact they make financial institution at the interest. Too many credit score playing cards simply spells trouble. If you need to pursue monetary freedom, remove as many credit score merchandise as you may.

Avoid Binge Shopping

I recognize that after I get depressed, I love to head shopping. When I see Some thing I like, I purchase it. It ' s most effective later that I remorse this selection. I examine my financial institution account and comprehend I simply didn ' t have the cash for that sort of shopping. That ' s after I both consume the price or go back the objects. Returning unplanned buys is embarrassing for me, so I have a tendency to take the monetary hit instead. So, when you have a spending addiction like mine, attempt to locate approaches that you may relieve your temper with out journeying a retail establishment!

Budget High

When I prepare my finances, I constantly finances greater than the real bill. By having this cushion, if some thing have to arise and I do must pay greater, than I ' m organized for it. This additionally allows me to make certain that I actually have sufficient to cowl the whole lot for the month.

Give Up Things

If you don ' t want it, then deliver it up. Being frugal isn ' t all approximately cash, however what you've got got in different possessions as properly. Having an excessive amount of could make your existence complex and cluttered. Learn to shed a few matters to stay fortuitously and frugally.

Avoid Credit

As stated earlIer than, credit score has an unsightly manner of sucking up your finances. By keeping off getting concerned in credit score, you're now no longer overpaying for the objects you purchase. I actually have keep credit score playing cards that I use to maintain my credit score excessive simply in case I want to apply it, however for the maximum part, if I don't have cash to shop for it, I
don't.

Learning approaches to lessen your debt will assist you to look extra cash on the cease of the month. If you don't have the cash, don't spend it! That is why maximum humans have a tendency to be in debt. They spend cash they don't have. By most effective getting what you want and now no longer the use of credit score to get there, you're to your manner to being frugal and seeing a high-quality cease result.

Chapter 5- New Habits for Changing the Way You Spend Money

It is probably a hard idea to extrade the way you spend your cash. After all, you earned it, So aren ' t you entitled to spend it how you'll like? Yes and no. While you do earn your cash, you need to be smart on how you operate it. Spending cash on stupid objects could be a waste. However, you notice humans doing this all of the time. They like it, in order that they purchase it. This finally ends up supplying you with a number of litter and now no longer sufficient cash. So, with the aid of using converting the way you view and spend your cash, you'll be properly to your manner to locating monetary freedom.

Think Twice Before Purchasing

It may also appear awkward for a while, however whilst you ' re thinking about shopping for some thing that might not be essential, take a step again and assume thru the scenarios. Will or not it's used? Is it beneficial in your existence? Can you do with out it? After answering a hard and fast of questions, then you'll be capable of make an knowledgeable selection approximately the potential buy.

Put Items Back

If you want to throw matters into the cart as you go, discover ways to glance through your cart and positioned at the least a 3rd of your cart again. If you've got got a listing and sticking to that listing, you then definately won't must fear approximately this step. However, in case you're simply happening the fly, you then definately probable have an excessive amount of for your cart.

Buy Only What You Need

When purchasing, make a listing and keep on with it. That manner, you're simplest shopping for what you want and now no longer something extra. If the temptation rises to shop for extra, maintain walking.

Treat Yourself Every Once in a While

Being frugal doesn't suggest doing with out. So, whilst you experience such as you want a touch pick-me-up, deal with your self to some thing which you enjoy. Don't completely deny your self definitely to store cash all of the time.

Use Cash Instead of Cards

I discovered that if I finances with cash, it's less difficult for me to now no longer spend extra. At the start of the month, I will set apart sufficient cash for gas, groceries, and some other component that I want. Once that cash is spent, it's long gone and I ought to wait till the following finances to shop for more. However, if it's a scenario of starving, I will bend that rule, however for the maximum part, it cuts down on extra spending while purchasing.

Use a Handbasket for Small Trips

When you already know which you simplest want some gadgets, take hold of a handbasket in place of a complete cart. This will restriction your temptation to throw gadgets which you don't want into the cart. I discovered that I actually have stored myself a whole lot of cash due to the fact I don't inventory up on needless gadgets.

Weigh the Pros and Cons of the Purchase

If it's a substantial buy, assume via it earlier than you purchase it. A sweet bar is one component even as a whole patio set is any other. Look on the complete photo of the buy. How will it's used and the way will it have an effect on your finances? By questioning via the buy, you're making it an knowledgeable choice instead of a spontaneous buy.

Know What Your Bank Accounts Look Like at All Times

If you operate a debit card, realize what you're spending and what kind of is on your account in any respect times. Banks are making this less difficult through having cellular apps so that it will inform you how a whole lot you've got got in any respect times. If you don't realize what you've got got, you run the hazard of overspending and accruing financial institution charges so that it will fee you even more.

Know When to Walk Away

If you already know that some thing isn't essential and which you can not come up with the money for it, learn how to step farfar from it and store it for any other day. Odds are which you're going to overlook which you desired it withinside the first area and now no longer even omit it.

Avoid Spontaneous Shopping Trips

Make certain which you're making plans your purchasing trips. This manner creating a listing and understanding about what you intend to spend at that unique area. This will come up with a guiding principle as to what you want in place of impulse shopping for.

By understanding and converting you spending behavior, you'll locate that your spending capabilities are certainly greater. You have manage of what you spend and what you purchase instead of an impulse which you remorse later. Take a terrific have a take a observe your spending behavior and spot what regions you may extrade a good way to make sure which you ' re now no longer spending cash unnecessarily.

Chapter 6- Learning to Only Buy What is Needed

In our society, we cost having as a whole lot as we probable can. However, this could harm each our shallowness and our pocketbooks if we ' re now no longer careful. Look round you. How a whole lot of what you notice is an absolute necessity? Not very a whole lot, I ' m guessing. While it ' s pleasant to have pleasant belongings, it could additionally motive you economic hardships looking to get to the factor wherein you experience like you may examine to others.

Learning to mention no to a number of the matters that you're feeling you must have takes time and discipline. It ' s now no longer impossible, though. You simply want to get into the dependancy of seeing what you want earlier than you buy it. In this chapter, I ' m going to provide you a few thoughts of a way to compare whether or not or now no longer you want some thing instead of definitely looking it.

Stop Before You Buy

When you ' re thinking about shopping for a positive item, prevent for a second and compare the entire photo. What are you going to use it for? Is there another way to avoid having to buy the new item? Is it priced too highly? Could you wait for a sale? Really take all of the options into perspective and make an informed decision on your purchases.

Evaluate Whether You Need the Item

You ' re at the shop and approximately to shop for some thing that has stuck your attention. However, you already know which you honestly don ' t want it and that it won ' t get a whole lot use. Would you be inclined to stay with out it? Is it essential in your life? Know what you ' re stepping into earlier than shopping for some thing so that it will take a seat down unused and emerge as being a waste of cash.

Putting Things Back

We stated this in a previous chapter. While shopping, in case you recognize that the acquisition is sheer impulse, positioned it again. You could instead do that while
you ' re in the shop in preference to whilst you ' re at domestic and are pressured to go back the object. It ' s plenty simpler to mention no earlier than buying than going again to the shop to go back an object!

Wish List vs. Need List

I actually have began out a brand new gadget in my household. When there may be some thing that catches our eyes, we've got lists that the object may be positioned on. The want listing consists of objects with a view to be essential and beneficial for the man or woman. The desire listing is the listing that consists of what the man or woman would love to have however they definitely don ' t want.

Know What is Needed Before Going right into a Store

There are many extraordinary approaches to make certain which you ' re shopping for simplest what is wanted whilst you visit a store. I actually have stated lists withinside the preceding chapters, however there also are techniques to hold own circle of relatives participants from setting matters that aren't wanted into the cart. In my household, we've got an know-how that we move via way of means of the listing and want to speak approximately something that appears to leap out at us while we're truely at the shop. That manner, monetary frugality is the duty of the complete own circle of relatives, now no longer simply the adults.

Another aspect I love to do is deliver the children an allowance. This is cash that they could spend as they sense essential. When that cash is long gone, then it ' s long gone till they obtain the following allowance. I agree with that this teaches them monetary duty and a way to store and spend their cash.

It is pretty vital which you recognize essential purchases in preference to useless purchases. With such a lot of extraordinary messages approximately what you want or want, it may get tough to recognize what is wanted in preference to a luxury. If you've got got problem telling the distinction among the, then suppose again in your fundamental needs. Think food, shelter, and safety and recognize what receives the ones for you. If you don ' t discover that it ' s essential to fulfill your fundamental needs, then it will become a desire in preference to a want.

Know what you want and purchase accordingly. It's k to deal with your self every
as soon as in a while, however you need to ensure which you're now no longer overdoing it on a everyday basis. Being frugal isn't approximately self-denial, however approximately getting to know self- control.

Chapter 7- Enjoying a Stress-free and Happy Financial Life

Once you recognize monetary freedom and residing frugally, you'll discover that it's miles nonetheless an exciting manner to live. Just due to the fact you don't have what anybody thinks you need to need to be glad doesn't suggest which you can not be glad. Once I reduce down on shopping for useless garbage, I discovered that I changed into capable of pay my payments extra effortlessly and now no longer need to fear approximately developing quick on the quit of the month. Having that monetary guarantee took away a huge quantity of strain in my life.

Worrying approximately your budget is one of the maximum worrying matters in life. Emergencies happen, we have a tendency to now no longer suppose via purchases, after which we discover ourselves dipping into our financial savings bills or borrowing cash from household or buddies to be able to meet our fundamental needs. If we had simplest concept via the monetary scenario earlier, we would have prevented the complete scenario.

Being clever together along with your cash is simply one manner that you could make a large effect in your monetary freedom. Many folks have debt. However, if we attention on getting rid of debt and residing inside our means, then we will revel in a happier lifestyle. If you discover which you're in a task wherein you're now no longer making sufficient to help even a easy lifestyle, don't forget converting jobs if possible. Your goals and strength of will are only a few of the elements which could make it a profitable extrade.

I'm now no longer telling you that that is going to be easy. For a few it'll be simpler for than others. However, there are numerous horrific spending behavior that human beings have that may be tough to extrade. Take your monetary behavior one dependancy at a time. Don't crush your self via way of means of seeking to make a couple of adjustments at as soon as. Habit stacking is a splendid idea that promotes extrade with out being beaten via way of means of it.

Have goals, however don't set your goals too excessive to start with. In order to construct lengthy and lasting behavior, you need to take adjustments in small steps. It is easy
to surrender on some thing due to the fact it's too hard. This is what occurs while we strive to tackle an excessive amount of at as soon as. Just don't forget that via way of means of taking one dependancy at a time which you're placing your self up for durable extrade in preference to utter failure.

After constructing a few wholesome frugal monetary desires in my home, I locate that the pressure degrees have long past down, making all people a whole lot happier. Everyone has a element in ensuring that the spending goes withinside the proper direction. Not handiest are we constructing wholesome monetary conduct as a family, however we're coaching our youngsters the obligations of money.

If you're geared up to make a few modifications so you are residing a greater frugal lifestyles, I inspire you to select a few wholesome conduct to pursue and start to paintings on them. It can handiest assist you to be greater liberated financially and decrease the pressure of residing paycheck to paycheck.

Good success to your pursuit of a wholesome and frugal monetary lifestyles!

Conclusion

Thank you once more for downloading this ee-e book!

I desire this ee-e book turned into capin a position that will help you to locate properly monetary conduct to construct with a view to reap frugality on your private lifestyles. Financial stresses are one of the most important issues that save you humans from being happy. However, it doesn't ought to be that manner. With some modifications in your mind-set and your conduct, you may be properly to your manner to monetary freedom.

The subsequent step is to become aware of the regions on your lifestyles wherein you want to extrade your spending conduct. Try the use of a number of the thoughts on this ee-e book that will help you extrade your conduct and your mind-set approximately money. Once you may construct nice monetary conduct, you'll be properly to your manner to overcoming debt and residing a happier and greater frugal lifestyle!

Finally, in case you loved this ee-e book, then I ' d want to ask you for a favor, could you be type sufficient to go away a evaluation for this ee-e book on Amazon? It ' d be substantially appreciated!

50 Ways to Declutter Your Space

Chapter 1- What is Too Much in Life?

Have you noticed that this society emphasizes success by how much you have rather than happiness? I have found that I hate the fact that my success is based upon how much I have. Sure, it is probably excellent to have the brand new devices and the whole lot you can in all likelihood need, however withinside the end, is it in reality really well worth it? No ownership or quantity of pastime can in reality fulfill your want for achievement.

Success is described in a different way for distinctive humans. Sure, a few would possibly thrive off of getting greater and greater. However, our human nature isn't based upon having extra. We have easy wishes that we want met, however past that, the whole lot is simply taken into consideration a luxury. When we make our luxuries into wishes, then we have a tendency to be unhappy.

I actually have evaluated my lifestyles and located that obtaining rid of the extras makes me sense happier. I'm now no longer harassed out with seeking to reap greater and what I actually have is sufficient. When I subsequently got here to that mind-set, it turned into a massive relief. I didn't sense like I had to do the whole lot with a view to accomplish a intention that wasn't even necessary.

How approximately you? Do you locate which you're harassed out via way of means of considering all you need to do with a view to keep what you've got got? Take a near study your lifestyles. Do you've got got extra which you're seeking to keep? Are there matters that you may do without? If your solution to any of those questions is " yes, " I inspire you to examine this ee-e book and reevaluate what's in reality a want rather than what's a luxury. What you may discover approximately your self would possibly wonder you.

If you're trying to simplify your lifestyles, I inspire you to hold reading. In this ee-e book, I'm going to present you a few pointers and guidelines on a way to put off the extra so you can revel in what you've got got. You would possibly locate that the easy lifestyles is the manner to head and like it as a whole lot as I do!

Chapter 2- Evaluating Need versus Want

The first step to locating a easy lifestyles is asking at what's earlier than you. Some matters you've got got you'll don't forget a want, at the same time as different matters are taken into consideration muddle and will without difficulty be achieved away with. For a few, they don't forget matters as wishes what others could without difficulty be capable of put off. Since every body is distinctive, I need to study the standards for what a want is rather than a need. I'm now no longer pronouncing it's incorrect to have gadgets you need. However, whilst your lifestyles turns into depending on retaining a sure preferred of lifestyles this is unnecessary, then it turns into a pressure for you and an inhibitor to the easy lifestyle.

So, I inspire you to be brutally sincere with your self whilst searching on the gadgets on your lifestyles. If you locate which you have greater of what you need than what you without a doubt want, you may need to reevaluate your priorities with a view to simplify your lifestyles.

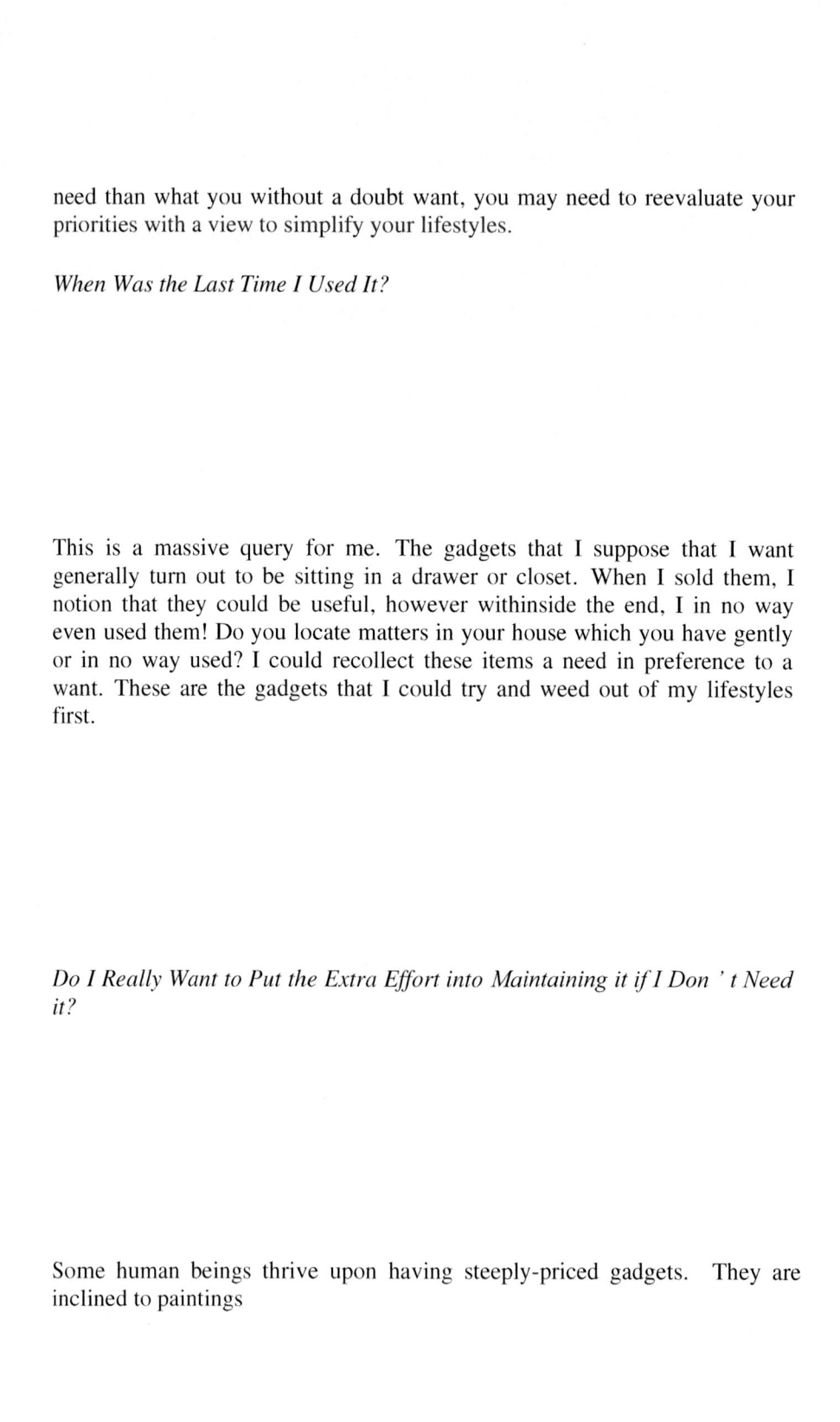

When Was the Last Time I Used It?

This is a massive query for me. The gadgets that I suppose that I want generally turn out to be sitting in a drawer or closet. When I sold them, I notion that they could be useful, however withinside the end, I in no way even used them! Do you locate matters in your house which you have gently or in no way used? I could recollect these items a need in preference to a want. These are the gadgets that I could try and weed out of my lifestyles first.

Do I Really Want to Put the Extra Effort into Maintaining it if I Don't Need it?

Some human beings thrive upon having steeply-priced gadgets. They are inclined to paintings tough for them, and they'll do anything they could to preserve them. However, a number of these items are simply now no longer really well worth the effort. For example, you've got got a automobile which you certainly like, however it has a tendency to interrupt down a lot. You spend quite a few money and time looking to preserve it in running order. When requested whether or not or now no longer you recollect this a want, you will say yes. So, you're inclined to position forth the more time and effort to hold your luxury. If it's far some thing which you actually need and could recollect a want, then through all means, preserve it.

If I have been to Toss it Out, Would I Miss It?

Before I determined to simplify my lifestyles and home, I could continuously encounter gadgets that I had no concept I even owned. They have been likely a few impulse purchase that I notion that I could use later. However, they quickly ended up getting saved and forgotten approximately. I want to invite myself after I come upon such gadgets one urgent query; " Will I pass over it if it have been now no longer here? " For maximum of these items, it might be a resounding " YES! " For others, I certainly did want it, however in the long run forgot to apply it. In a busy, cluttered lifestyles, that occasionally happens.

Does it Make Me Happy?

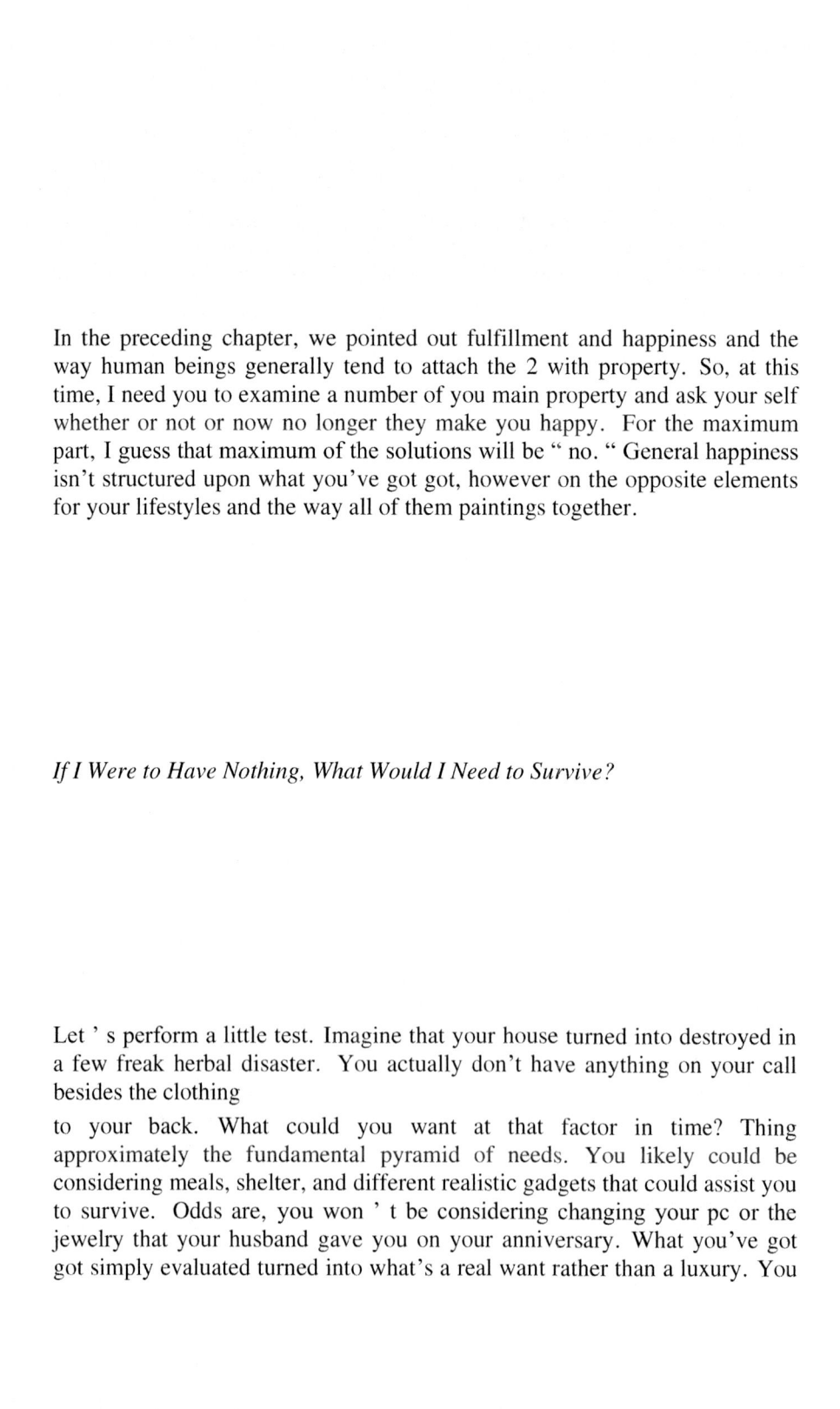

In the preceding chapter, we pointed out fulfillment and happiness and the way human beings generally tend to attach the 2 with property. So, at this time, I need you to examine a number of you main property and ask your self whether or not or now no longer they make you happy. For the maximum part, I guess that maximum of the solutions will be " no. " General happiness isn't structured upon what you've got got, however on the opposite elements for your lifestyles and the way all of them paintings together.

If I Were to Have Nothing, What Would I Need to Survive?

Let ' s perform a little test. Imagine that your house turned into destroyed in a few freak herbal disaster. You actually don't have anything on your call besides the clothing

to your back. What could you want at that factor in time? Thing approximately the fundamental pyramid of needs. You likely could be considering meals, shelter, and different realistic gadgets that could assist you to survive. Odds are, you won ' t be considering changing your pc or the jewelry that your husband gave you on your anniversary. What you've got got simply evaluated turned into what's a real want rather than a luxury. You can stay with out a pc laptop and jewelry. You can ' t stay with out meals or shelter.

The subsequent time you go searching your house, ask your self a number of those questions. You is probably amazed on the sheer quantity of products which you personal which you certainly should stay with out. Try creating a extrade to a easy lifestyles through removing the luxuries and focusing at the needs. In the subsequent chapters, I ' m going to offer you pointers on a way to simplify your lifestyles in some one of a kind ways. Items aren't the best matters that preserve us from revel in easy living!

Chapter 3- How to Reduce Your Belongings

As highlighted withinside the preceding chapter, our property have a tendency to be the primary element that continues us from having a easy lifestyles. Even aleven though they may be simply stuff, we generally tend to shape emotional bonds with these things that may be tough to interrupt. However, it is probably vital to interrupt those bond if you ' re trying to simplify your lifestyles. This can take the time and endurance to your part. No one desires to admit that Some thing that they certainly like is not anything greater than a element. So, I ' m going to offer you a few pointers and pointers on a way to lessen your property a good way to stay a happier lifestyles.

Go Through Everything You Own

Depending upon how plenty you own, this will be pretty the undertaking. However, it is going to be vital for you to downsize your property to a possible level. The first element that I suggest is which you undergo every and each object you own. Take a near have a take a observe them, and separate them into piles. Have a pile for what you'll for certain preserve, one for the maybes, and one to put off. Do this room through room in order that your property won ' t seem like a complete and entire wreck. The objects that you could thoroughly say which you want to preserve may be positioned returned proper away and you could compare the relaxation of it later on.

Evaluate whether or not what you've got got earlier than you is needed

This is a check of your will. Take a while and have a take a observe your stuff. Ask your self whether or not or now no longer you actually need the object and whether or not or now no longer you'll ever use the object on a everyday basis. Imagine how your existence could be with out it. If you could thoroughly say which you simply don ' t want it, put off it. It ' s higher to be sincere with your self and do it unexpectedly than locating out later which you saved some thing round that ended in litter.

Donate or Sell Your Excess Stuff

This is every other vital component for your puzzle. Now is the time to put off the objects which you have determined which you don't want. I favor to donate them to a thrift keep or have a storage sale. For a few, donating it's miles the perfect option. For me, I experience having a every year storage sale and casting off things. Not simplest does it make me money, However I additionally have the risk to ask pals or own circle of relatives to deliver their stuff and it's like a reunion. However, arranging a storage sale may be time eating and traumatic in case you don't pass approximately it withinside the proper manner.

Have Someone Help You

Some humans refuse to are searching for assist. However, in case you're residing with others, they want to be at the equal web page as you, so enlisting their assist can be vital. Even in case you stay alone, having a pal come over and assist you to put off a few useless stuff can each be a laugh and helpful. You in no way know, your buddy would possibly simply take a number of that stuff off of your fingers for you and that's one much less fear later on!

Asking for assist isn't always a signal of weakness. It's genuinely pronouncing which you need to make a alternate and which you need every other individual to be part of that alternate. So, don't fear approximately a person wondering you're vulnerable for requesting assist. You're simply looking to do what's exceptional for you.

Give it to Family or Friends

Having younger (or older) siblings may be every other a laugh manner to put off your undesirable property. For me, I actually have a sister who loves my tastes in apparel and domestic dé cor, so after I requested if she desired to return back over and take a number of the objects I become casting off, she become excited. You would possibly have a pal who's like that for you. Knowing a person who stocks your tastes is a great manner to recycle a number of the antique stuff you must put off. If you've got got a few own circle of relatives or pals who would like to alleviate you of your extra property, don't be afraid to invite them! It may want to advantage each of you.

Be Heartless

This is one tip that has helped me alongside the manner. Since I base loads of emotional price on a number of my property, after I visit put off them, I locate that I doubt my choice primarily based totally upon that bond. It can be some thing that I were given with my mom that brings returned recollections. However, that is some thing I should appearance beyond. Look on the object for what it's miles. Will you want it or use it? Can you stay with out it? Be heartless and rip the recollections which can be related to item farfar from it. In the end, it's simply a chunk of stuff a good way to litter your domestic. Remember that!

If You Haven't used it in Six Months, Trash it

Another amazing approach that I use to declutter my domestic is to have a take a observe what's earlier than me and compare whether or not or now no longer I actually have used this object withinside the beyond six months. If I haven't used or checked out it that long, I haven't neglected it. I will positioned it into my donation pile. The largest mistake that you could make is to have a take a observe the item and inform your self that you'll use it again. You won't, so don't preserve it round. Six months is an inexpensive time span to understand whether or not or now no longer you'll in reality use it.

Downsize Your Home

For a number of us, we stay in a domestic this is plenty too huge for our needs. If
Possible, downsize your residing quarters to some thing this is extra plausible to easy and furnish. I recognize that transferring isn't always viable for all, however when you have the possibility to downsize your home, you'll additionally be pressured to take away a number of your assets whilst you move. Think approximately it. This is probably the manner to go!

Downsizing your possessions may be a hard and time eating manner. No one loves to take away their matters. After all, you selected them and labored tough to shop for them. However, while your lifestyles turns into complex due to your want to keep your possessions, you ' re now no longer going to be happy. Try decluttering and downsizing withinside the vicinity of your possessions and notice how lots higher you sense via way of means of making this change.

This is a manner. Don't crush your self with removing all of the objects you don't want at once. This will make the complete concept appear even extra overwhelming than simply retaining the stuff to your lifestyles. So, I advise which you take this manner in pieces. It ought to take you some months to make it through. However lengthy it takes, recognise which you're creating a high-quality step closer to simplifying your lifestyles with the losing of your extra possessions.

Chapter 4- Cutting Back on Your Chore List

Another accurate manner to inspire easy residing is via way of means of slicing lower back at the listing of factors that you are feeling you need to have completed. People generally tend to place an excessive amount of on themselves, making it extra tough to have time for what genuinely topics. Depending in your way of life and personality, you'll price a while differently. If you sense like you're spending an excessive amount of time doing mundane chores, then perhaps it's time to reevaluate your priorities and find time for what genuinely topics as opposed to filling a while with nonsense.

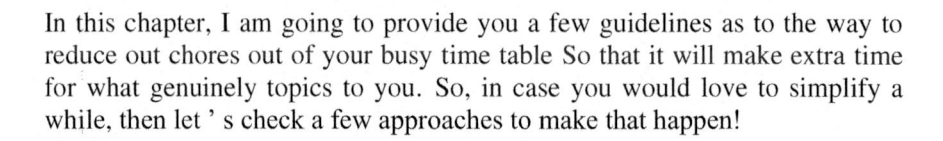

In this chapter, I am going to provide you a few guidelines as to the way to reduce out chores out of your busy time table So that it will make extra time for what genuinely topics to you. So, in case you would love to simplify a while, then let's check a few approaches to make that happen!

Does it Really Need to be completed?

Some obligations are vital so that it will run your household. Others are absolutely fillers. When you examine your day and the listing which you have compiled which you need to get completed, consider whether or not or now no longer the undertaking ought to get completed so that it will keep your lifestyles, or if it's some thing which you pick out to do. By being sincere with your self and figuring out which you're selecting up an excessive amount of in your to do listing, you'll be in your manner to pronouncing that a few obligations are useless and muddle a while.

Can You Have Someone Else do it?

When did it grow to be a reality which you do all of the chores? If you stay with

a couple of humans, that is unfair and worrying to you. Take a examine your day instead of the others you stay with. Can a perSon else do the undertaking at the listing? If you ' re like me and try and do it all, then there may be truly a person who might be capin a position that will help you via way of means of taking up the undertaking and finishing it. So, the following time you sense beaten via way of means of the to do listing, consider this factor. Have a person assist you!

What Would you do with Some Free Time?

Feel unfastened to daydream a touch bit. What might you do in case you discovered a few greater unfastened time inside your day? Well, via way of means of simplifying your chore listing, you is probably capable of make this daydream a possibility. Don ' t be afraid to think about how you would spend your time if you didn ' t have a million things to do. It can genuinely workout that you could have that point in case you discover ways to control a while nicely and omit useless obligations.

What Activities Would You Like to Spend Your Time Doing?

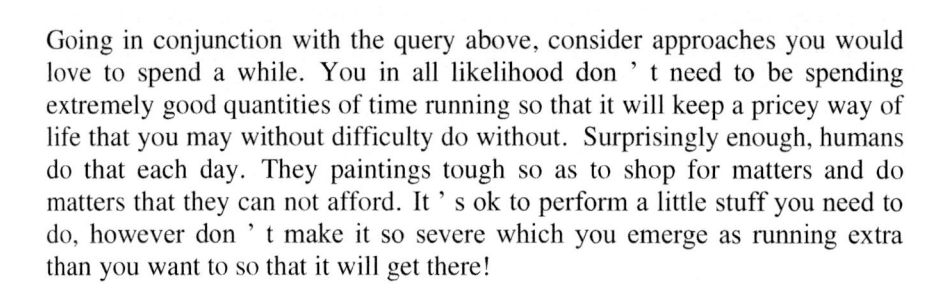

Going in conjunction with the query above, consider approaches you would love to spend a while. You in all likelihood don't need to be spending extremely good quantities of time running so that it will keep a pricey way of life that you may without difficulty do without. Surprisingly enough, humans do that each day. They paintings tough so as to shop for matters and do matters that they can not afford. It's ok to perform a little stuff you need to do, however don't make it so severe which you emerge as running extra than you want to so that it will get there!

Respect Your Time and That of Others

In today's world, we appearance out for primary and try and consciousness on supporting anybody else on the identical time. If you're this sort of humans, you'll give

some time to assist every body in want. This may be a advantageous thing, however it is able to without problems grow to be some thing negative. People who recognise that you'll do some thing you need them to do will use you for that reason. They may have little regard in your time, however awareness on what you could do for them. On the turn side, you is probably that man or woman who expects that from others. The largest tip I can provide right here is appreciate your personal time and that of others. Once you research that some time is treasured and their time is too, you may be locating that you could hold a more fit stability on your time table.

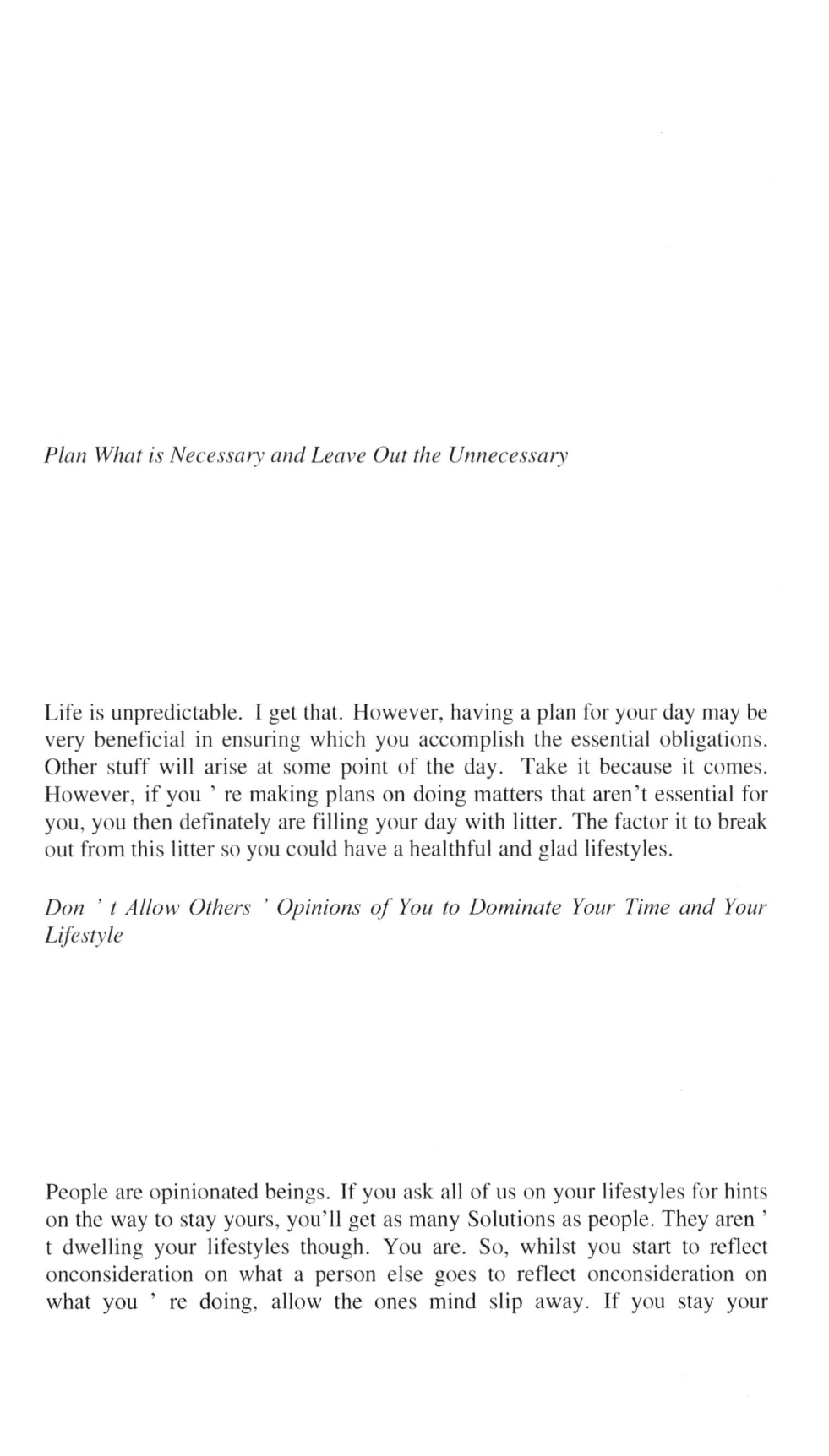

Plan What is Necessary and Leave Out the Unnecessary

Life is unpredictable. I get that. However, having a plan for your day may be very beneficial in ensuring which you accomplish the essential obligations. Other stuff will arise at some point of the day. Take it because it comes. However, if you ' re making plans on doing matters that aren't essential for you, you then definately are filling your day with litter. The factor it to break out from this litter so you could have a healthful and glad lifestyles.

Don ' t Allow Others ' Opinions of You to Dominate Your Time and Your Lifestyle

People are opinionated beings. If you ask all of us on your lifestyles for hints on the way to stay yours, you'll get as many Solutions as people. They aren ' t dwelling your lifestyles though. You are. So, whilst you start to reflect onconsideration on what a person else goes to reflect onconsideration on what you ' re doing, allow the ones mind slip away. If you stay your lifestyles primarily based totally upon a person else ' s critiques, you ' re now no longer dwelling your personal lifestyles, however theirs. Let them stay the manner they need and also you stay the manner you need. Don ' t permit different people ' s critiques to dictate the way you stay your lifestyles.

By making a few modifications for your time table and what you pick out to do on a day by day basis, you could simplify your lifestyles and make your self happier due to the fact you'll have extra time to do what you need to do. Your time table is a massive a part of your day, so being capable of reduce out the useless elements will make it simpler with a purpose to have time for what you would love to do and spend time with folks that you value.

Time is a elaborate thing. We discover ourselves losing it often after which wishing we should have it back. If you discover which you have a tendency to waste extra time than the usage of it productively, try and make a few modifications for your time table with a view to open up time for what's essential and what you will experience doing.

Chapter 5- Simplifying Your Thought Life

If you ' re something like me, then your thoughts is usually walking on overdrive. When I ' m now no longer considering one thing, any other concept consumes my thoughts. There isn't anyt any peace whilst you are continuously thinking. Have you ever attempted to simplify your mind so you could have a non violent existence? It is impossible, however you'll want to learn how to educate your mind to make it happen. This may be executed in some of ways, however relying on the way you operate, you would possibly discover one manner works plenty higher than any other.

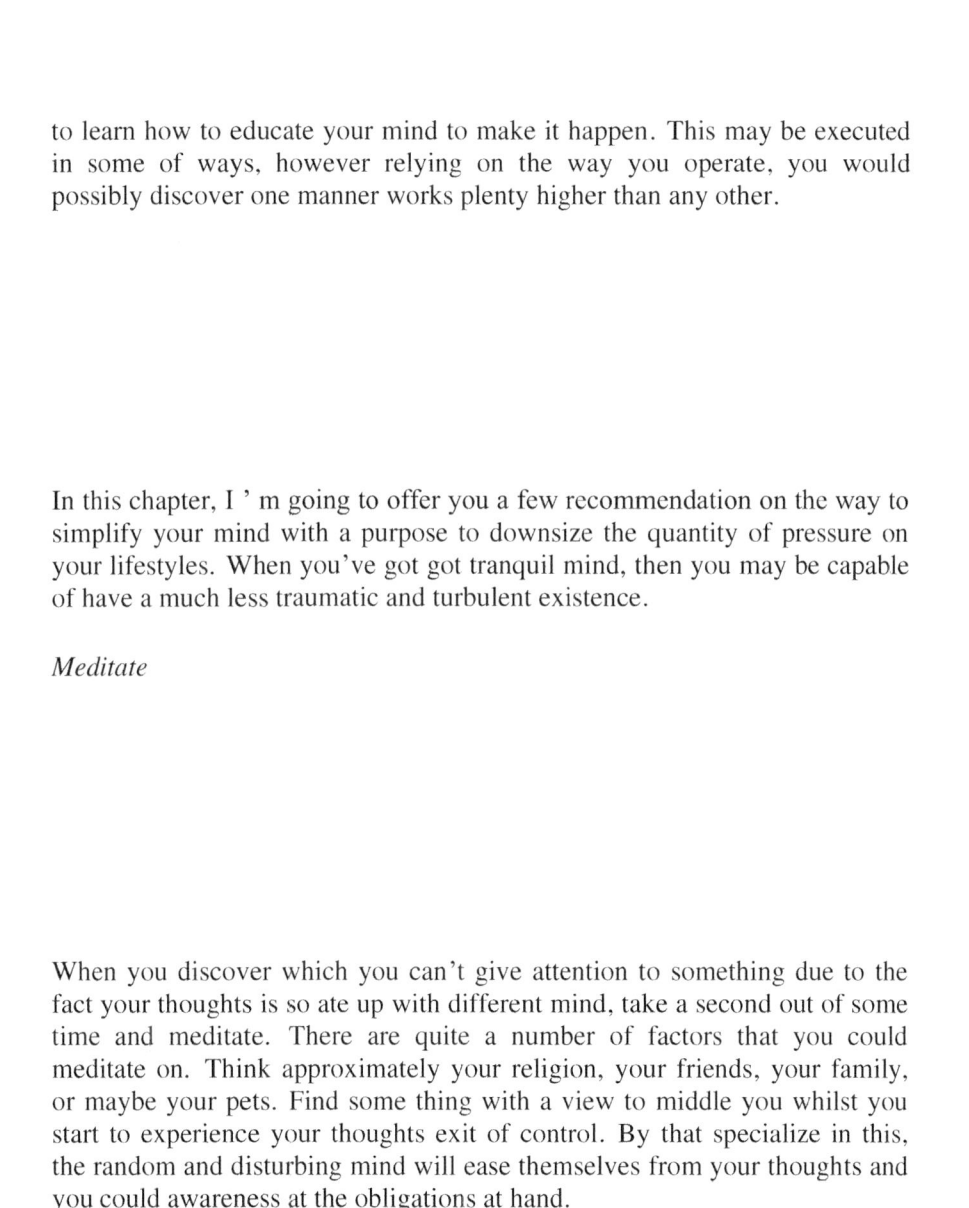

In this chapter, I'm going to offer you a few recommendation on the way to simplify your mind with a purpose to downsize the quantity of pressure on your lifestyles. When you've got got tranquil mind, then you may be capable of have a much less traumatic and turbulent existence.

Meditate

When you discover which you can't give attention to something due to the fact your thoughts is so ate up with different mind, take a second out of some time and meditate. There are quite a number of factors that you could meditate on. Think approximately your religion, your friends, your family, or maybe your pets. Find some thing with a view to middle you whilst you start to experience your thoughts exit of control. By that specialize in this, the random and disturbing mind will ease themselves from your thoughts and you could awareness at the obligations at hand.

Prayer

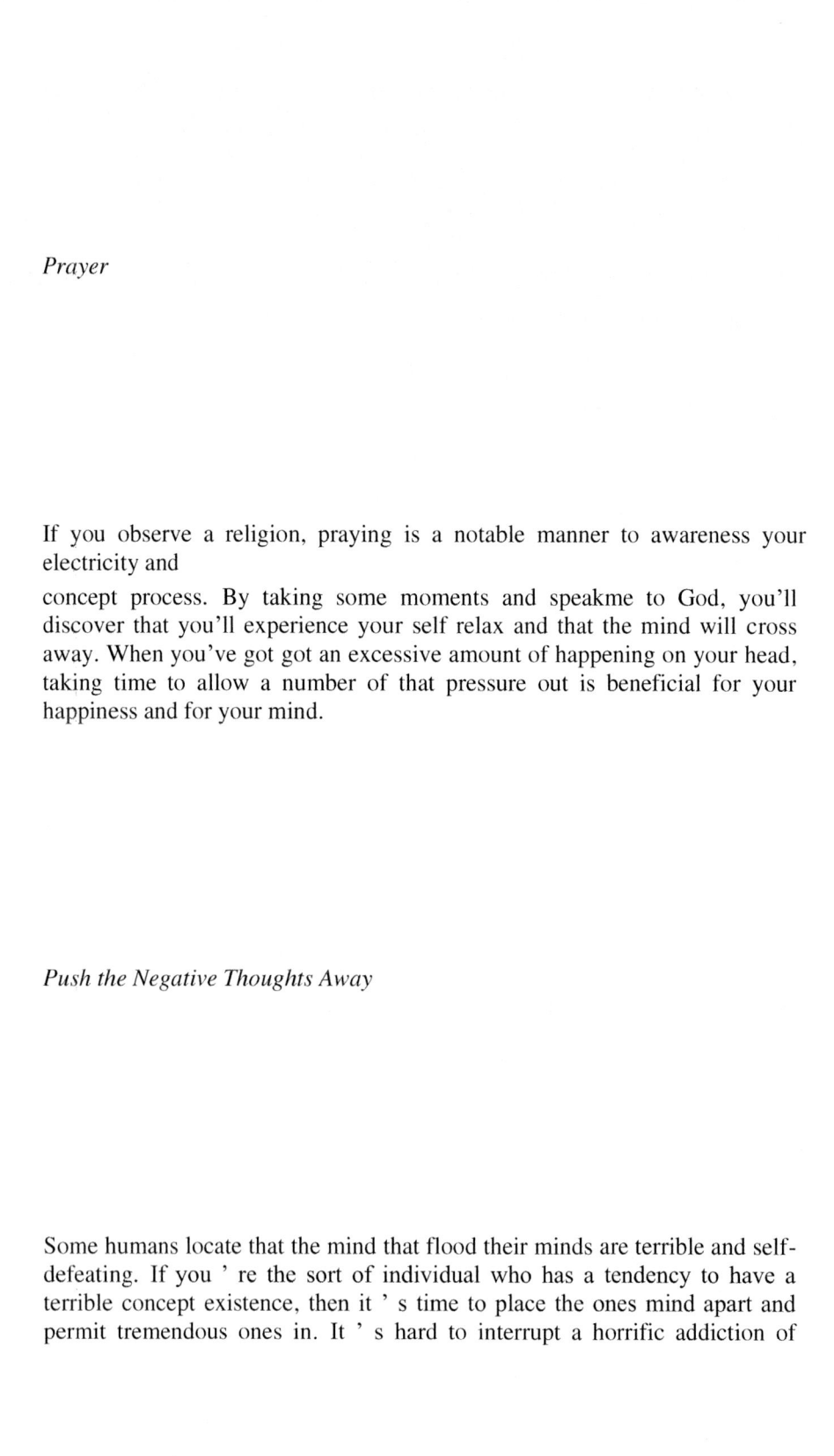

If you observe a religion, praying is a notable manner to awareness your electricity and

concept process. By taking some moments and speakme to God, you'll discover that you'll experience your self relax and that the mind will cross away. When you've got got an excessive amount of happening on your head, taking time to allow a number of that pressure out is beneficial for your happiness and for your mind.

Push the Negative Thoughts Away

Some humans locate that the mind that flood their minds are terrible and self-defeating. If you ' re the sort of individual who has a tendency to have a terrible concept existence, then it ' s time to place the ones mind apart and permit tremendous ones in. It ' s hard to interrupt a horrific addiction of terrible wondering as soon as it begins. However, attempt to interrupt the sample with the aid of using pushing the ones terrible mind from your head and seeking to update them with happier mind. You will in no way have a satisfied existence in case your thoughts is cluttered with the aid of using terrible mind!

Focus at the Moment

Focus is one of the approaches that you may make your concept approaches less complicated and greater pleasurable. I locate that I generally tend to permit my thoughts wander whilst the subject of my awareness isn ' t thrilling or concept-provoking. However, if I have been to awareness at the moment, I might get that project achieved faster after which I might have time to reflect onconsideration on different matters. If you lack awareness on what you want to do, then you'll simplest draw out the manner and make it longer than it without a doubt desires to be.

Push Away the " What if " Mentality

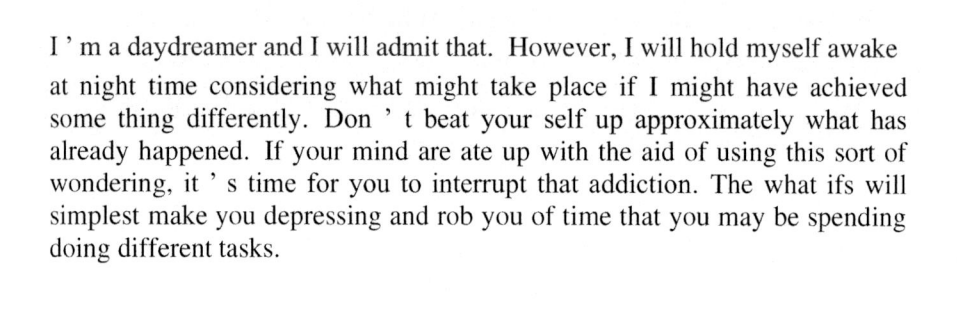

I'm a daydreamer and I will admit that. However, I will hold myself awake at night time considering what might take place if I might have achieved some thing differently. Don't beat your self up approximately what has already happened. If your mind are ate up with the aid of using this sort of wondering, it's time for you to interrupt that addiction. The what ifs will simplest make you depressing and rob you of time that you may be spending doing different tasks.

Stop Random Thinking When it Begins

If your thoughts has a tendency to wander, then attempt to forestall it from going to locations it doesn't want to be earlier than it has a threat to move there. There are positive triggers so one can get me to begin considering random circumstances. Once I diagnosed those triggers, I turned into capable of forestall the random mind earlier than they even had a threat to begin. Think approximately matters so one can divert your interest and apprehend them when you have problem that specialize in what desires to be achieved. Knowing those diversions will make it less complicated with a view to push them away whilst vital.

Learn to Say No to Your Thoughts

Sometimes, random mind do creep in. You begin with the aid of using asking your self whether or not or now no longer you must pass and do an pastime later on. Before you already know it, you may be considering doing this pastime, the ramifications of the pastime, what it'll entail, and any quantity of mind that surround it. However, you ' re prepurported to be targeted on any other project. That project is being disregarded to your random mind. So, learn the way to mention no on your mind whilst you observe that they could lead you down a direction so one can cause distraction. If the concept is important, jot it down and are available returned to it if you have time to reflect onconsideration on it.

Life has a tendency to be greater complex whilst we suppose greater than we must approximately matters we shouldn ' t be considering. We all do it. Depending on the way you take care of the mind and pick to remove them will decide your thoughts ' s declutter manner. Yes, your thoughts may be simply as cluttered as your agenda or your home. By gaining knowledge of to simplify your concept manner, you'll find out that you'll have greater freedom to get what desires to be achieved achieved and feature time to do what you would really like to do afterwards.

Thoughts are a hard territory to control. We are used to our mind taking us anyplace they need to, and attempting to inform them they could ' t do this may be a protracted and irritating manner. However, you'll locate that simplifying your mind will growth your capacity to guide a easy and happier lifestyle.

Chapter 6- Enjoying what Matters

If you've got got observed which you don't have an awful lot time to experience your existence, then it's pretty feasible which you have an excessive amount of stuff going on. Whether it's an excessive amount of stuff or too many mind, some thing is making it so you can't experience what without a doubt subjects to you. It may make an effort to determine out what's making your existence so complex and stressful, however when you do, you may be capable of make the vital modifications with a view to stay a less complicated, greater pleasurable existence.

After discussing the way to rid your self of all of the greater stuff for your existence, I'd want to take this bankruptcy to awareness on the way to experience what subjects to you as soon as you've got got cleared out the litter of existence. Again, this is probably a degree so one can make an effort to reach, however when you're there, you may be happier and greater fulfilled together along with your existence.

Plan Fun Activities with Those You Care About

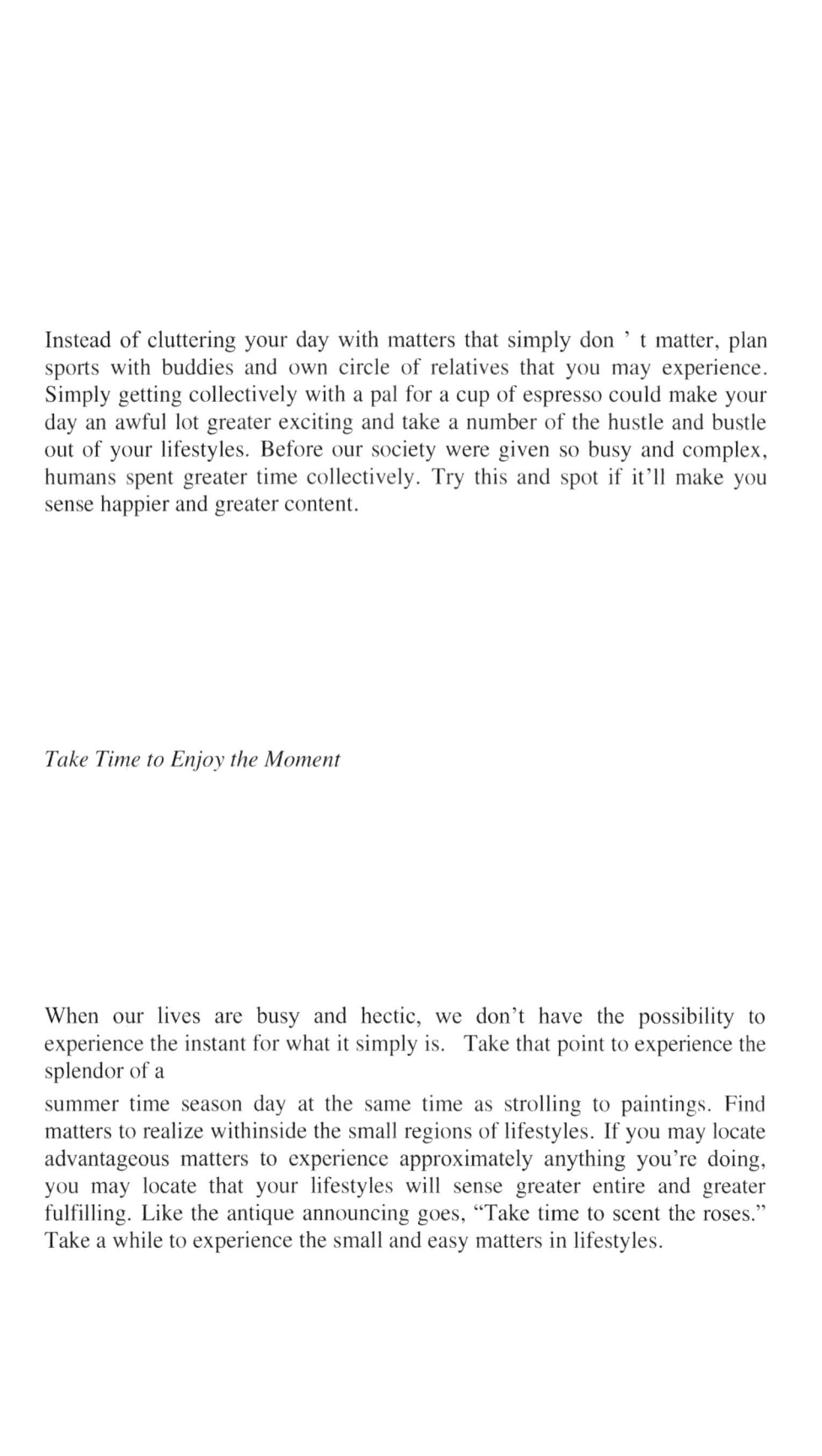

Instead of cluttering your day with matters that simply don ' t matter, plan sports with buddies and own circle of relatives that you may experience. Simply getting collectively with a pal for a cup of espresso could make your day an awful lot greater exciting and take a number of the hustle and bustle out of your lifestyles. Before our society were given so busy and complex, humans spent greater time collectively. Try this and spot if it'll make you sense happier and greater content.

Take Time to Enjoy the Moment

When our lives are busy and hectic, we don't have the possibility to experience the instant for what it simply is. Take that point to experience the splendor of a

summer time season day at the same time as strolling to paintings. Find matters to realize withinside the small regions of lifestyles. If you may locate advantageous matters to experience approximately anything you're doing, you may locate that your lifestyles will sense greater entire and greater fulfilling. Like the antique announcing goes, "Take time to scent the roses." Take a while to experience the small and easy matters in lifestyles.

Take Time for What You Want to Do

You may sense which you're being egocentric via way of means of doing this, however via way of means of taking time to do what you experience will have a large effect for your lifestyles. This may be a easy issue which you experience doing on a day by day foundation to help you to experience your day. Maybe you want the greater flavored creamer to your espresso, so that you use it while you sense like you would possibly have a hard day. Whatever you need to do, deliver your self the pride of doing it. It will assist you to experience your lifestyles greater.

Don't Allow Others to Dominate Your Time

We talked a bit approximately this in a preceding chapter. If you're the kind of man or woman who will bend over backwards to assist a person, you may get taken benefit of via way of means of the incorrect humans. When that happens, they may dominate it slow with their desires and also you won't have time to attend to your very own desires. This isn't always handiest robbing you of it slow, however it additionally permits them to apply others in place of being self-sufficient. Don't be afraid to mention no to a person who manifestly can fend for himself. You aren't being cruel, you're simply making it so you will have it slow and the opposite man or woman will discover ways to do for himself.

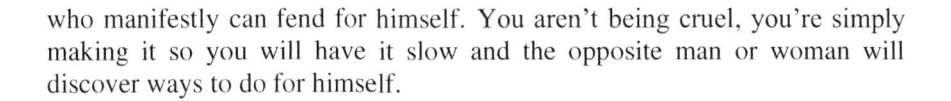

Allow Yourself the Freedom to Enjoy Your Time

I recognize that I locate myself feeling responsible once I get time to myself. I continually sense like I will be doing some thing else to assist a person else. However, if I don't appearance out for myself, then I am in the long run walking myself closer to a situation of being burnt out. Take a while to do what you experience and deliver your self the liberty to experience that point with out feeling responsible. Sadly enough, maximum people don't get that freedom in our lives, and it's far essential to hold ourselves glad and centered.

Learning to experience the modifications which you make to your lifestyles is critical to creating your easy lifestyles paintings for you. If you're making modifications for your lifestyles and that they pass with out notice, then you definitely have wasted it slow. So, while you pursue that easy lifestyles, discover ways to locate methods to experience your lifestyles. Like I said above, you may definitely experience a stroll out of your automobile for your region of employment. It's the easy matters in lifestyles that simply make it greater exciting.

One of the most important limitations that you may bear whilst seeking to experience it slow is the sensation of guilt which you're now no longer supporting a person else. The quicker you recognize which you want to attend to your self earlier than you may assist others, the earlier you may be loose to experience a easy lifestyles and love it.

Chapter 7- Loving Your Simple Life

Life isn't intended to be complex and stressful. We make it that manner with what we pick out to do with our lives. So, via way of means of understanding that your lifestyles doesn't need to be complex, you're geared up to pursue a easy and exciting lifestyles!

Now which you're for your manner to locating out how a easy lifestyles can advantage your manner of questioning and the way you stay your lifestyles, you may start to taking part in your easy lifestyles. Since you're so used to creating selections primarily based totally upon a hectic and complete lifestyles, having time to experience the easy matters in lifestyles is probably new idea to you. What might you do if you may take a breath and experience lifestyles for what it's far?

Let me inform you a touch bit approximately my very own experience. Now that I don't have the pressure of offering a way of life past my means, I am a good deal happier. I love the truth that I don't should fear approximately how I'm going to pay my bills, what I want to buy, and who will choose me for my easy lifestyles. Since I even have discovered that we generally tend to position on a display for the relaxation of the sector, now no longer doing so has made a large effect on how I experience my lifestyles. It's my lifestyles and nobody else's reviews matter.

Once you're taking the following step and recognize which you don't want the sector to be happy, you'll be to your manner to locating your happiness. By casting off all of the extra, you're honestly gaining extra. You can have extra time, extra exceptional for your relationships, and much less pressure. Those all sound great, right?

If you haven't notion approximately pursuing a less complicated way of life, then I inspire you to offer it a try. There are many humans I recognize of who're taking the following steps to casting off the extra of their lives and I can already see a distinction of their lives. They simply appear happier and extra fulfilled.

Take the danger at being happy. Downsize and spot how it may gain you. I'm dwelling a easy way of life and loving it, and I'm certain you may too if you may deliver it a danger. Good luck!

Conclusion

Thank you once more for downloading this ee-e book!

I wish this ee-e book turned into capin a position that will help you to locate approaches to simplify your lifestyles thru casting off useless thoughts, possessions, and chores. We generally tend to make our lives a good deal extra complex with out which means to. By having a easy lifestyles, we are able to discover ways to experience our lives a good deal extra.

The subsequent step is to parent out regions to your lifestyles which might be complex. By understanding what you would love to extrade approximately your lifestyles, you'll be organized to take steps to simplify your day and love it!

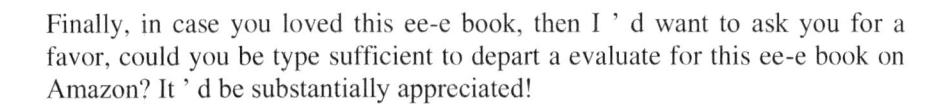

Finally, in case you loved this ee-e book, then I'd want to ask you for a favor, could you be type sufficient to depart a evaluate for this ee-e book on Amazon? It'd be substantially appreciated!

Simple Living and Loving It

Have you ever notion approximately what it might be like in case you had much less stuff and extra time to experience the matters you adore to do? If your lifestyles has emerge as too cluttered and too complex, then it is able to be time to simplify your lifestyles. By casting off the matters that make you experience as aleven though you don't have any time, you may now no longer handiest simplify your lifestyles, however will experience like you've got got extra time to spend at the matters that definitely matter. Give those 50 steps a try to see wherein it may lead you!

Thanks once more for downloading this ee-e book, I wish you experience it!

Chapter 1- How Did My Life Get So Complicated?

Life has a manner of having farfar from us with out us even figuring out it. It begins offevolved with choosing up extra obligation at paintings, shopping for a brand new home, having youngsters, and some of different matters that could purpose the easy matters to experience some distance away. Sometimes, you locate your self looking youngsters gambling at a park and marvel what passed off to that carefree sort of lifestyles. When did your lifestyles get so complex?

Take a study the youngsters you spot gambling withinside the park. What do they've which you don't? They appear to don't have any concerns and no stresses. How are you able to locate your manner again to that mentality? We all need to have that carefree feeling that we skilled as youngsters. You may marvel if there's ever a opportunity of having that again.

As adults, we generally tend to tackle increasingly more. Never thoughts the truth that we experience harassed out and it feels as aleven though the sector desires extra out of us. In order to get beforehand in lifestyles, it feels as aleven though we ought to take at the more paintings and obligation. However, have you ever ever notion approximately simplifying your lifestyles so you can decrease the pressure and concerns that plague your day?

With increasingly more needs on our time, it'd appear not possible to locate relaxation from the stresses of each day lifestyles. Our society has emerge as notably insistent on getting extra performed in much less time. However, have you ever notion approximately approaches to decrease the stresses that the sector places on you and your time?

If you're like maximum humans, a touch peace and quiet among the chaos sounds great. Let's take this adventure collectively and find out the way to simplify our lives and locate extra peace and amusement in small matters. In this ee-e book, I'm going to offer you a few steps and hints on the way to simplify your lifestyles so you can experience much less pressure and extra amusement.

Chapter 2- Steps for Simplifying Your Day

If you're like maximum of the human beings withinside the global today, your every day recurring is regularly stuffed and extra regularly than now no longer, you grow to be now no longer having the ability to perform the whole lot you had set out do. When all is stated and done, you experience like you've failed at your day due to the fact you didn't end the whole lot. What if the hassle wasn't which you didn't end, however which you attempted to do an excessive amount of in a single day? Maybe it's time to simplify your every day recurring so you don't experience pressured and annoyed with the unending listing of chores earlier than you.

Simplifying your day can do loads to treatment your strain degree and making you experience like you've completed what you got down to do. If you % an excessive amount of in, then it's time to discern out a way to do away with a number of the litter on your day. In this chapter, I'm going to present you a few realistic steps on a way to simplify your every day recurring so you experience much less pressured out and extra fulfilled whilst your day involves an end.

Prioritize What Really Needs to be Accomplished

If you discover that your to do listing is a mile lengthy and you realize which you're now no longer going to have sufficient time to finish it, take a second and plan out your day. Take a have a take a observe your time table and choose out which duties are maximum vital for you to finish. All of the opposite objects for your listing can look forward to every other day or every other time. Try taking the pinnacle 5 objects for your listing that you are feeling want to be completed and awareness on them. Once the ones are complete, you could pick out to finish different duties as appropriate.

Have a Set Schedule

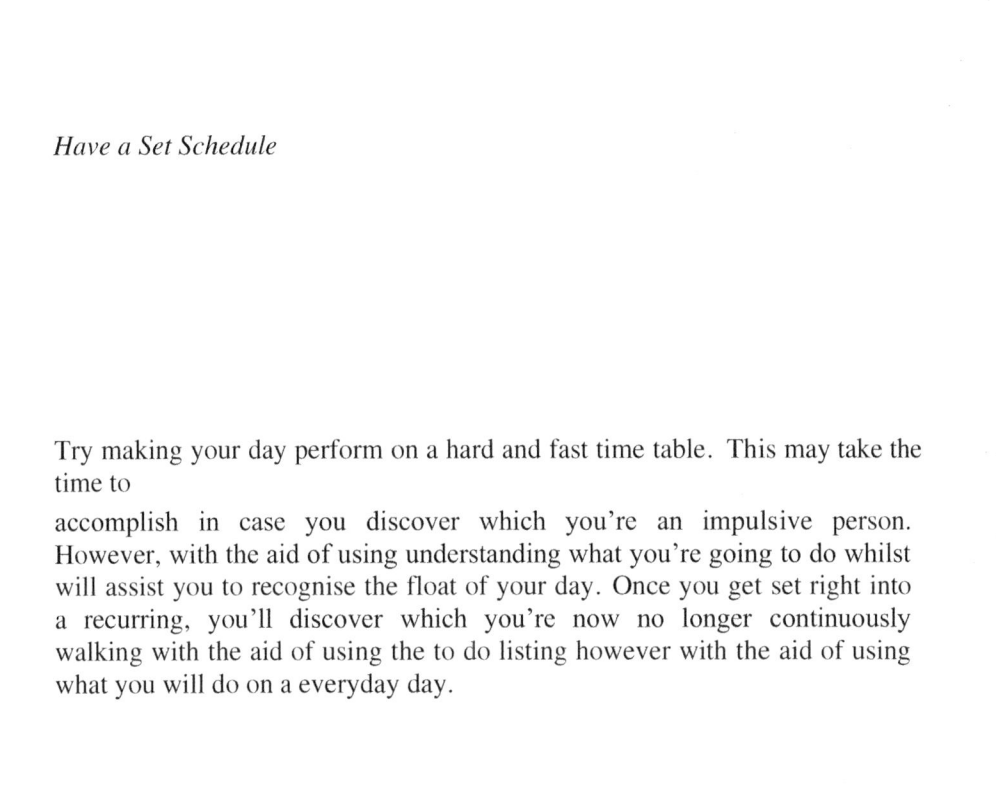

Try making your day perform on a hard and fast time table. This may take the time to
accomplish in case you discover which you're an impulsive person. However, with the aid of using understanding what you're going to do whilst will assist you to recognise the float of your day. Once you get set right into a recurring, you'll discover which you're now no longer continuously walking with the aid of using the to do listing however with the aid of using what you will do on a everyday day.

Ask for Help

There isn't anyt any disgrace in asking others to lend you a hand. If you discover which you have an excessive amount of for your plate, ask a person to assist. This can be as easy asking your partner to choose up the youngsters from football exercise or to choose up dinner at the manner domestic. Asking for assist will take the strain off of you and your time table and you may experience like extra gets completed inside a given day.

Get Rid of Unnecessary Projects

Have you ever observed which you attempt new matters which you see on TV or the laptop which you do not forget great? If those tasks are useless in your every day living, then it's now no longer essential to pursue them. Just as it seems neat doesn't suggest that you need to pursue it. I recognise that my existence receives slowed down with the aid of using the random tasks that I choose up alongside the manner. Sometimes those tasks bring about litter, which takes extra of my time to smooth up. A few craft tasks with the youngsters is one thing, however taking up a brand new interest simply as it seems neat can take some time and your area away.

Simplify Your Tasks at Home

Is your private home existence so packed complete of to dos which you discover which you don't even recognise what domestic definitely seems like? If your private home has emerge as an area to eat, sleep, and wash your clothing, then you're now no longer definitely taking part in a satisfying domestic existence. Home wishes to be an area of consolation and family. Therefore, take the time and make your recurring at domestic replicate that. Having a time table and a chore listing for whilst you're at domestic can substantially assist you to experience extra time collectively whilst absolutely each person is at domestic.

Learn How to Tell People No

If you want to assist others, then they may begin to come to you every time they discover themselves in want. Pretty soon, you may be doing extra for others than you may be doing for your self or your family. While it's great to assist others out, there must be a restriction to how plenty you could assist and also have a satisfied existence of your own. Don't experience terrible when you have to inform some human beings "no" with a purpose to find time for your self. If your buddies are certainly buddies, they may apprehend which you want to position your existence and wishes earlier than all of us else's.

Put the Phone Away

As a whole lot as we adore having the arena at our fingertips, having a phone with us always has a tendency to be a distraction. Since telephones provide extra features, you notice human beings with them of their palms or on their ears everywhere. Take a second to reflect onconsideration on what it changed into like earlier than mobileular telephones have been a big a part of society. People had extra time and extra attention on their lifestyles and what they wanted. Now, the telecellsmartphone can ring anywhere, at any time, and we sense obligated to answer. Try placing your telecellsmartphone away for an afternoon or maybe 1/2 of an afternoon and spot how a whole lot extra you could accomplish.

Allow Plenty of Time to Achieve Tasks

Once you've got got a listing of priorities in place, then you could plan round them. Since there are uncontrollable elements that inhibit our time, ensure which you permit sufficient time to perform your responsibilities and now no longer try and % an excessive amount of into your agenda. If you've got got an excessive amount of deliberate with too little time, a visitors jam or some other occasion could make it so you can not accomplish it all. I realize that once I can not accomplish what I got down to do, I get pissed off and discouraged. Therefore, ensure which you permit sufficient time to ensure you could whole what you got down to do.

Once you've got got a each day recurring full of precedence responsibilities, you may discover that you may have a extra fun day. Simplifying what you need to do and what sort of time you permit to do it'll make it viable to do extra of what you need to do. Take the time to prioritize your day each morning. Look on the pinnacle 5 stuff you ought to get finished and permit lots of time to get the ones finished. If you discover that a person else places a call for to your time, sense unfastened to both accommodate them or to inform them which you can not do it that day. Knowing what you're doing and what sort of you intend to get finished will make your day appear much less overwhelming and simpler.

I inspire you to attempt to agenda an afternoon with simplest 5 crucial responsibilities that

you ought to accomplish. Schedule while you plan to do them and what sort of time you need to take for them. Once the ones responsibilities are completed, then you could pursue different responsibilities of much less importance. Since you probably did now no longer plan for them, they may now no longer sense like a stressor upon you or some time. Simplify your day and the relaxation will fall into place.

Chapter 3- Steps for Downsizing

Do you discover which you spend a number of some time seeking to ensure that your property is clean, your garden is groomed, or that your automobile remains in order? Maybe you've got got an excessive amount of to attend to attempting to attend to your super-sized lifestyles. Would it's possible to downsize your property, your yard, or another a part of your lifestyles that appears too big? Even locating a manner to get a few help looking after your super-sized lifestyles could assist in relation to the strain department. Looking at the alternative aspect of the picture, you may have a small domestic and a small yard, however you've got got such a lot of property that it seems like you're filled in.

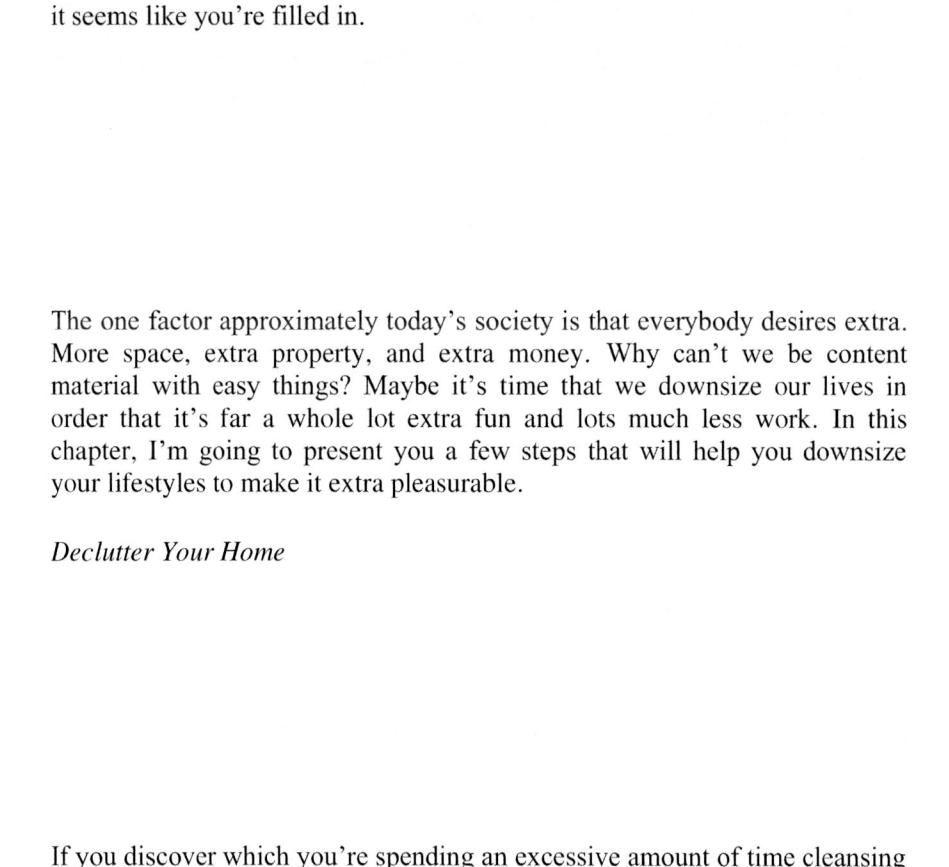

The one factor approximately today's society is that everybody desires extra. More space, extra property, and extra money. Why can't we be content material with easy things? Maybe it's time that we downsize our lives in order that it's far a whole lot extra fun and lots much less work. In this chapter, I'm going to present you a few steps that will help you downsize your lifestyles to make it extra pleasurable.

Declutter Your Home

If you discover which you're spending an excessive amount of time cleansing up the severa possessions you've got got acquired, it's an awesome time to declutter your property. Take a while and take away the gadgets which you don't have any realistic use for. Keep simplest what you operate on a each day foundation or are crucial and provide the relaxation away. Once you've got got much less in your property, you'll be capable of revel in what's maximum crucial to you.

Live in a Smaller House or Apartment

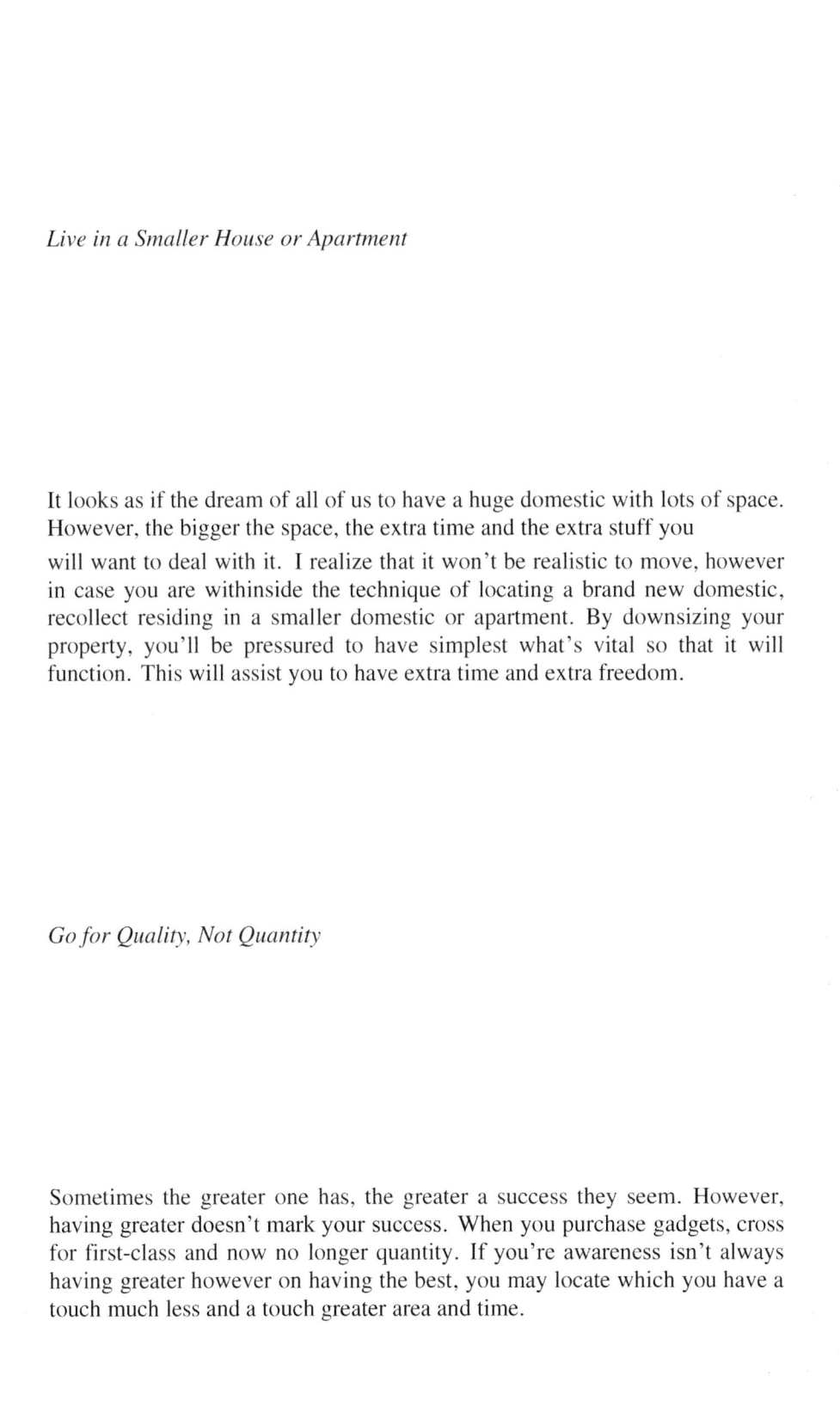

It looks as if the dream of all of us to have a huge domestic with lots of space. However, the bigger the space, the extra time and the extra stuff you
will want to deal with it. I realize that it won't be realistic to move, however in case you are withinside the technique of locating a brand new domestic, recollect residing in a smaller domestic or apartment. By downsizing your property, you'll be pressured to have simplest what's vital so that it will function. This will assist you to have extra time and extra freedom.

Go for Quality, Not Quantity

Sometimes the greater one has, the greater a success they seem. However, having greater doesn't mark your success. When you purchase gadgets, cross for first-class and now no longer quantity. If you're awareness isn't always having greater however on having the best, you may locate which you have a touch much less and a touch greater area and time.

Know Which Tasks to Eliminate from Your Day

When you awaken withinside the morning, you would possibly sense as aleven though you've got got one million matters that want to get performed. However, are they all important to get performed in a single day? If it's now no longer extraordinarily critical, positioned it at the listing for every other day or get rid of it altogether.

Downsize Your Wardrobe

How lots of your garments have sat for your closet for years with out you sporting them? If you locate which you have garb which you haven't worn in a protracted time, it's time to purge them out of your existence. Having fewer garments will assist simplify your choice on what you will put on whilst you get dressed.

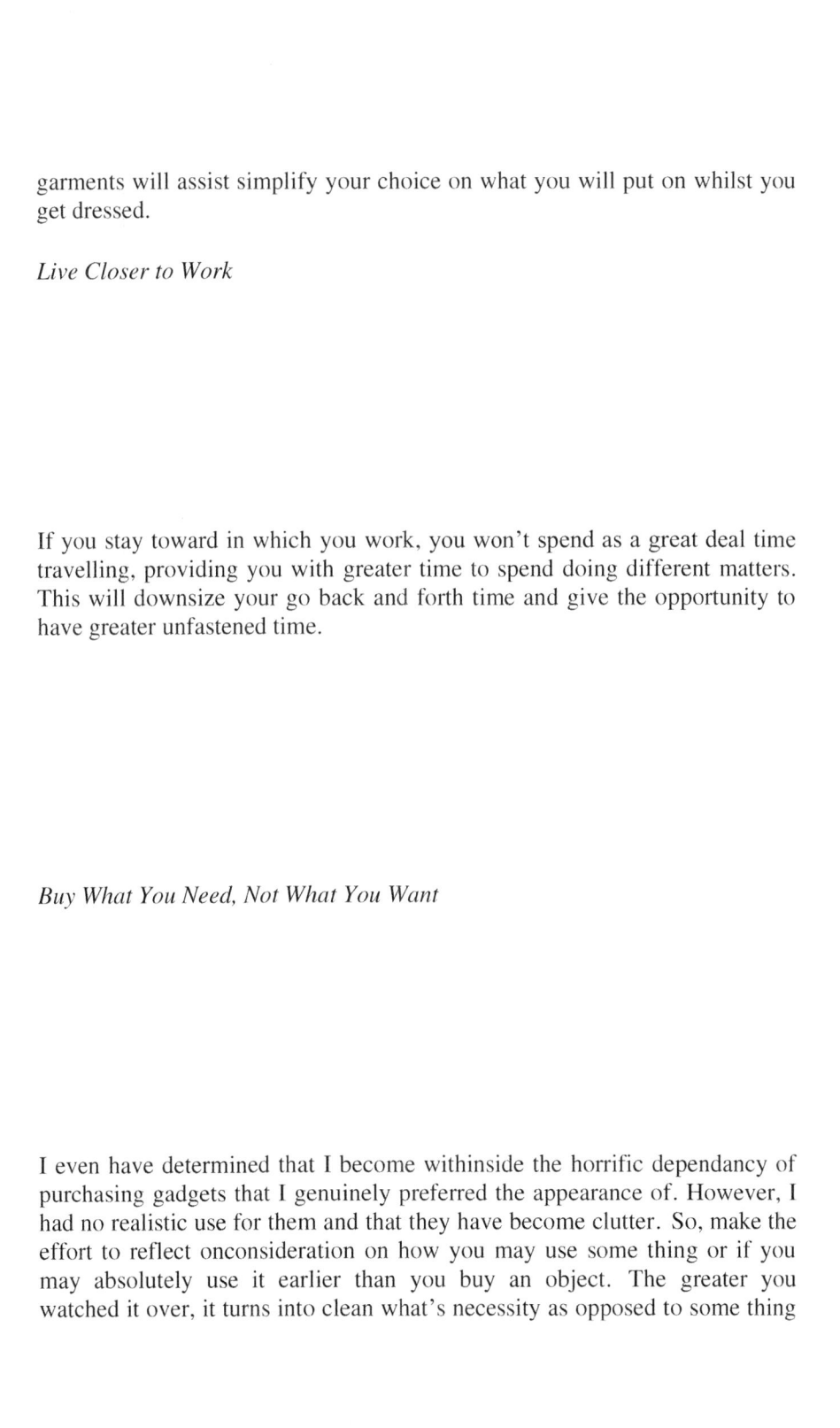

Live Closer to Work

If you stay toward in which you work, you won't spend as a great deal time travelling, providing you with greater time to spend doing different matters. This will downsize your go back and forth time and give the opportunity to have greater unfastened time.

Buy What You Need, Not What You Want

I even have determined that I become withinside the horrific dependancy of purchasing gadgets that I genuinely preferred the appearance of. However, I had no realistic use for them and that they have become clutter. So, make the effort to reflect onconsideration on how you may use some thing or if you may absolutely use it earlier than you buy an object. The greater you watched it over, it turns into clean what's necessity as opposed to some thing that's a need.

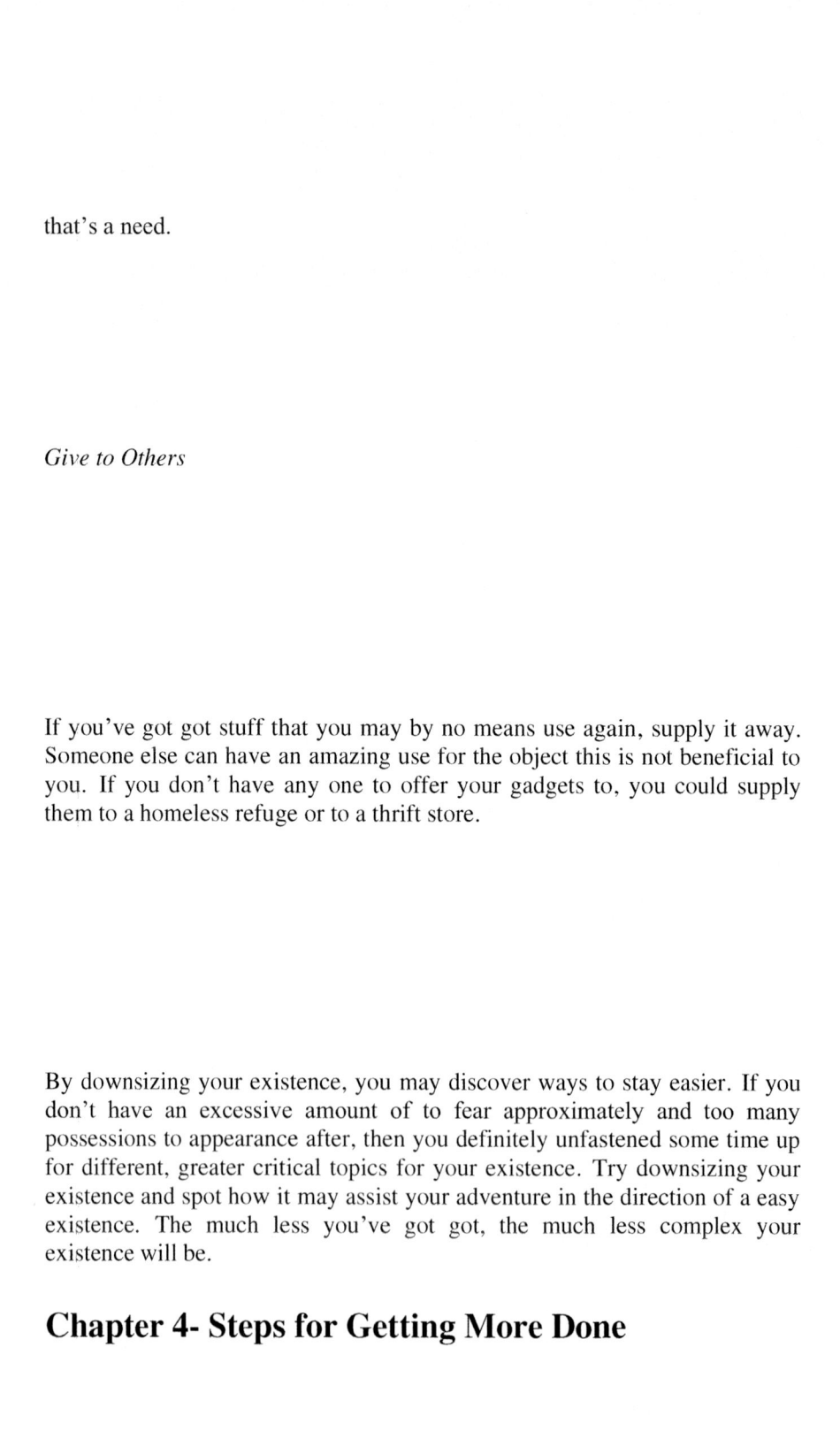

Give to Others

If you've got got stuff that you may by no means use again, supply it away. Someone else can have an amazing use for the object this is not beneficial to you. If you don't have any one to offer your gadgets to, you could supply them to a homeless refuge or to a thrift store.

By downsizing your existence, you may discover ways to stay easier. If you don't have an excessive amount of to fear approximately and too many possessions to appearance after, then you definitely unfastened some time up for different, greater critical topics for your existence. Try downsizing your existence and spot how it may assist your adventure in the direction of a easy existence. The much less you've got got, the much less complex your existence will be.

Chapter 4- Steps for Getting More Done

Have you determined which you nevertheless have a listing of to dos whilst the day is over with? If you've got got ever wanted for only a few greater hours withinside the day, then you definitely're now no longer the simplest one. Time has a manner of having farfar from us, and if we're now no longer careful, we turn out to be now no longer getting what we need performed. Just reflect onconsideration on what it'd be want to recognize which you finished the entirety you desired to get performed and also have a while for yourself. Well, there are methods that you could accomplish this. If you discover ways to simplify your duties, then you'll be capable of get greater performed and also have greater time to experience what you need to. Let's check a few steps to help you to get greater performed via way of means of simplifying your mission listing.

Think of Easier Ways to Accomplish Your Tasks

Sometimes, I locate that I make a mission a great deal greater hard than it absolutely desires to be. If there's a easier manner to perform a mission, then why now no longer do it that manner? For example, in case you locate it hard to run all your errands due to in which the locations are located, why now no longer attempt locating locations which might be inside nearer proximity so you can accomplish your duties in a shorter duration of time. The equal may be real of family duties. Try to consider less difficult methods to perform what you want to get performed and spot how a great deal greater you could do together along with your time!

Make a Plan

If you do matters as you reflect onconsideration on them, then you definitely greater than probable will neglect about to do some thing or spend time doing matters which might be pointless. Try taking off your day via way of means of making plans it out. Figure out what the maximum critical duties are and lead them to a concern whilst blockading out some time and whilst you will do them. By creating a plan, you may recognize what you're doing and whilst you are doing it. This will maintain you from doing pointless duties via way of means of considering doing it at the cross.

Weed Out Unnecessary Tasks

Along with the ultimate step, putting off pointless duties will come up with greater time to get the matters performed that want to be performed. Some duties that we make priorities don't really want to be on the the front of our minds. Keep in thoughts what are the critical duties and what may be brushed aside or prevented completely.

Enlist Other's Assistance

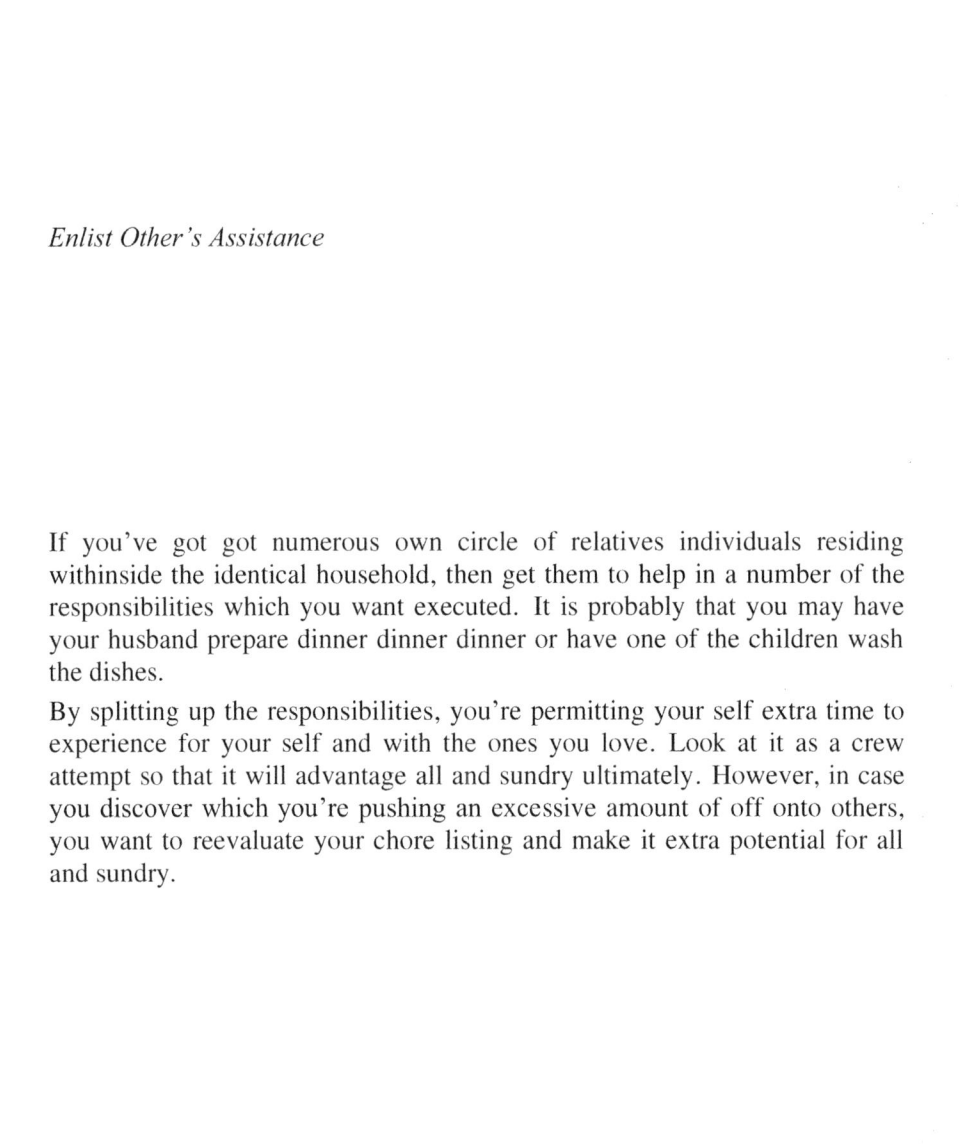

If you've got got numerous own circle of relatives individuals residing withinside the identical household, then get them to help in a number of the responsibilities which you want executed. It is probably that you may have your husband prepare dinner dinner dinner or have one of the children wash the dishes.

By splitting up the responsibilities, you're permitting your self extra time to experience for your self and with the ones you love. Look at it as a crew attempt so that it will advantage all and sundry ultimately. However, in case you discover which you're pushing an excessive amount of off onto others, you want to reevaluate your chore listing and make it extra potential for all and sundry.

Make Time for What's Important

Even while it seems like there isn't sufficient time to do the whole lot and nonetheless discover time for what you sense is essential, push different matters apart and find time for what's essential. Every man or woman has a exceptional listing of factors that they discover to be extra essential than others. Sometimes you need to time table time for them. If your time table is so loopy which you're lacking out on what's essential in lifestyles, then you definitely really want to weed out a few matters and make that point count.

If you're withinside the state of affairs wherein you need to get extra executed and feature extra time to spend with others, then attempt simplifying some time and your listing of what

wishes to get executed. When you've got got a listing of priorities, then you definitely are capable of delegate some time higher and recognise if you have loose time. Don't allow the hustle of the day manage you and some time. Take price your self.

Chapter 5- Putting it Into Practice

It's clean for us to make a listing of gadgets and steps that we would really like to have manifest in our lives. However, with out movement, there may be honestly no factor in having a vision. The factor I'm seeking to make right here is that we want to position those steps into movement with a purpose to make our dreams a reality. Let's test a few sensible approaches to ensure which you're try at a easy lifestyles can grow to be a concrete addiction.

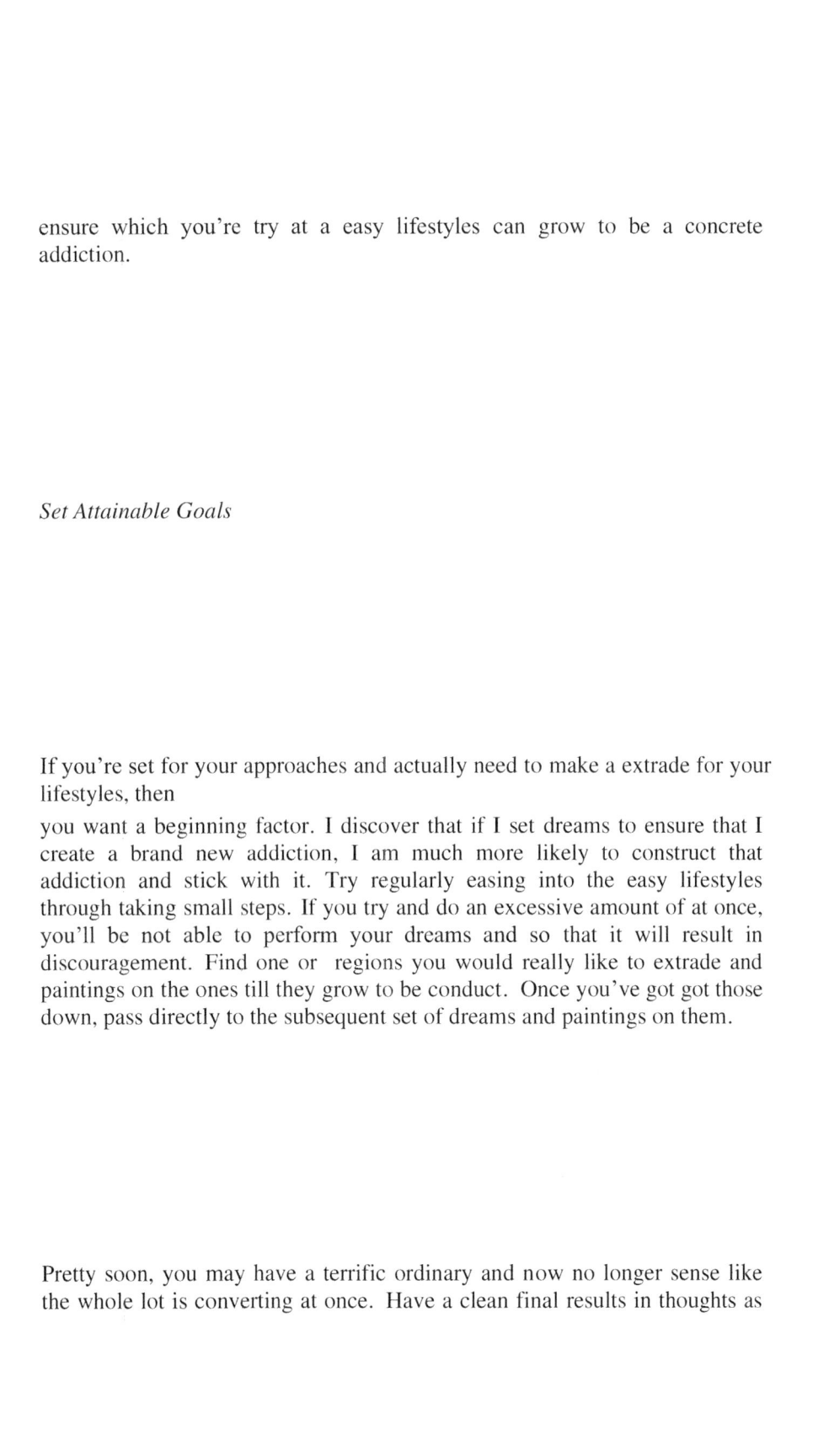

Set Attainable Goals

If you're set for your approaches and actually need to make a extrade for your lifestyles, then

you want a beginning factor. I discover that if I set dreams to ensure that I create a brand new addiction, I am much more likely to construct that addiction and stick with it. Try regularly easing into the easy lifestyles through taking small steps. If you try and do an excessive amount of at once, you'll be not able to perform your dreams and so that it will result in discouragement. Find one or regions you would really like to extrade and paintings on the ones till they grow to be conduct. Once you've got got those down, pass directly to the subsequent set of dreams and paintings on them.

Pretty soon, you may have a terrific ordinary and now no longer sense like the whole lot is converting at once. Have a clean final results in thoughts as you figure at the dreams and recognise wherein you need to be ultimately.

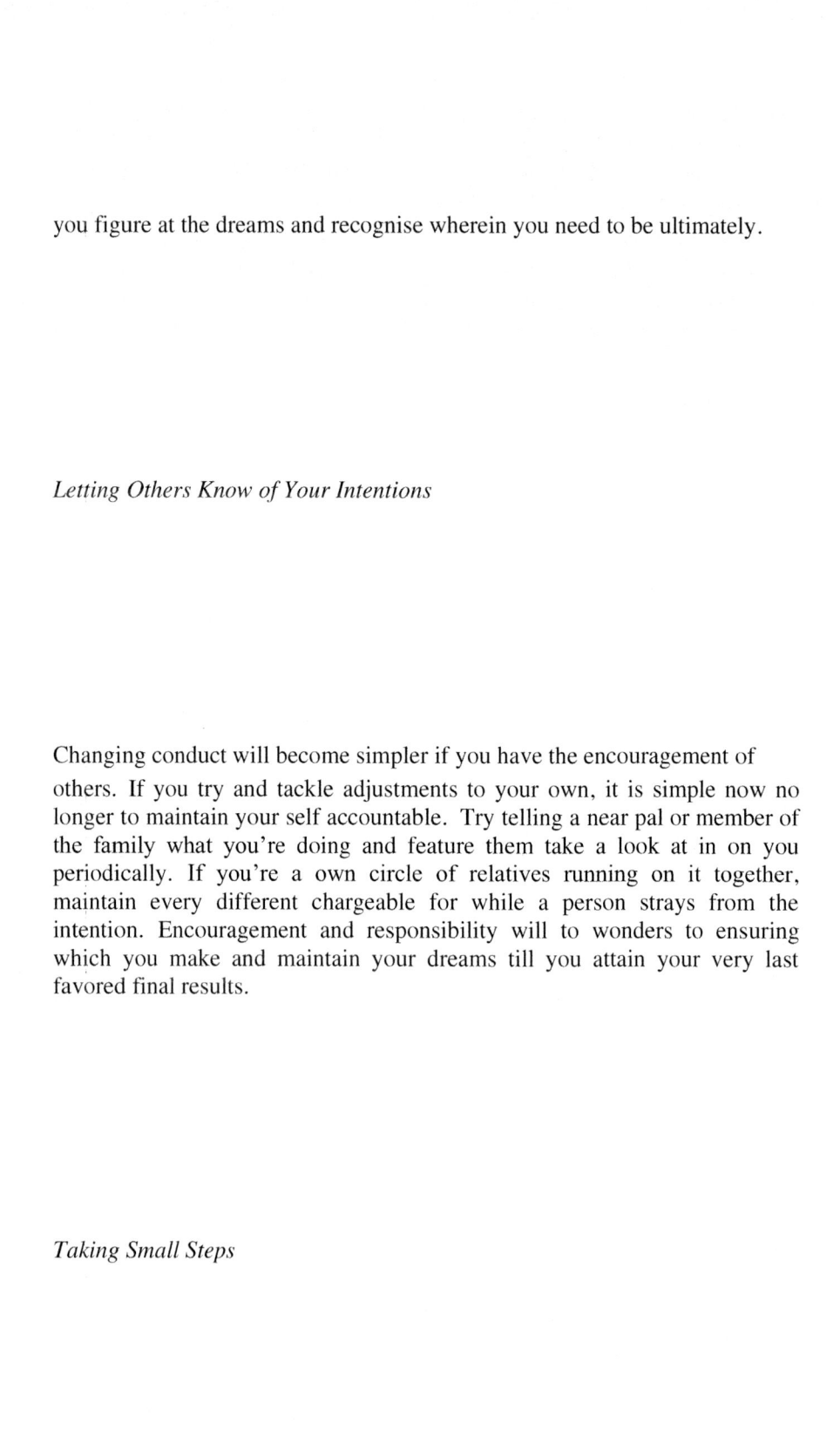

Letting Others Know of Your Intentions

Changing conduct will become simpler if you have the encouragement of others. If you try and tackle adjustments to your own, it is simple now no longer to maintain your self accountable. Try telling a near pal or member of the family what you're doing and feature them take a look at in on you periodically. If you're a own circle of relatives running on it together, maintain every different chargeable for while a person strays from the intention. Encouragement and responsibility will to wonders to ensuring which you make and maintain your dreams till you attain your very last favored final results.

Taking Small Steps

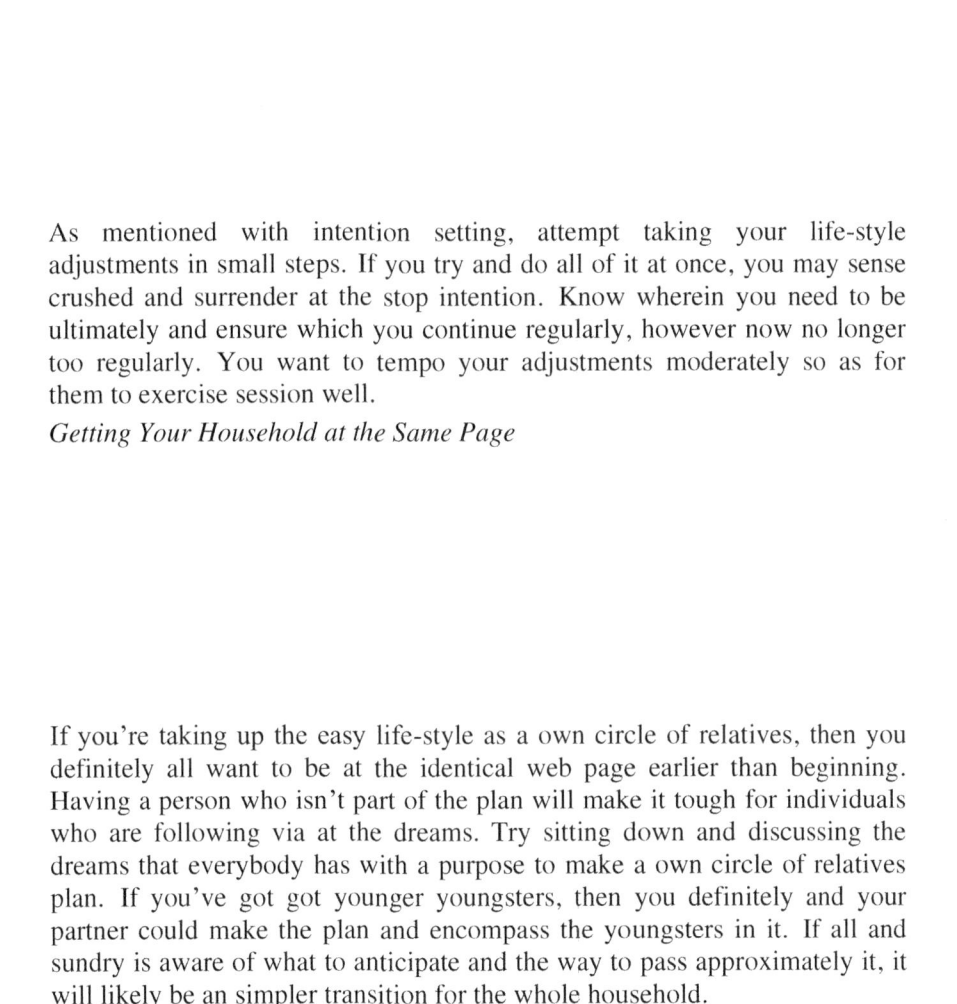

As mentioned with intention setting, attempt taking your life-style adjustments in small steps. If you try and do all of it at once, you may sense crushed and surrender at the stop intention. Know wherein you need to be ultimately and ensure which you continue regularly, however now no longer too regularly. You want to tempo your adjustments moderately so as for them to exercise session well.

Getting Your Household at the Same Page

If you're taking up the easy life-style as a own circle of relatives, then you definitely all want to be at the identical web page earlier than beginning. Having a person who isn't part of the plan will make it tough for individuals who are following via at the dreams. Try sitting down and discussing the dreams that everybody has with a purpose to make a own circle of relatives plan. If you've got got younger youngsters, then you definitely and your partner could make the plan and encompass the youngsters in it. If all and sundry is aware of what to anticipate and the way to pass approximately it, it will likely be an simpler transition for the whole household.

Keeping at it When It Doesn't Seem to be Working

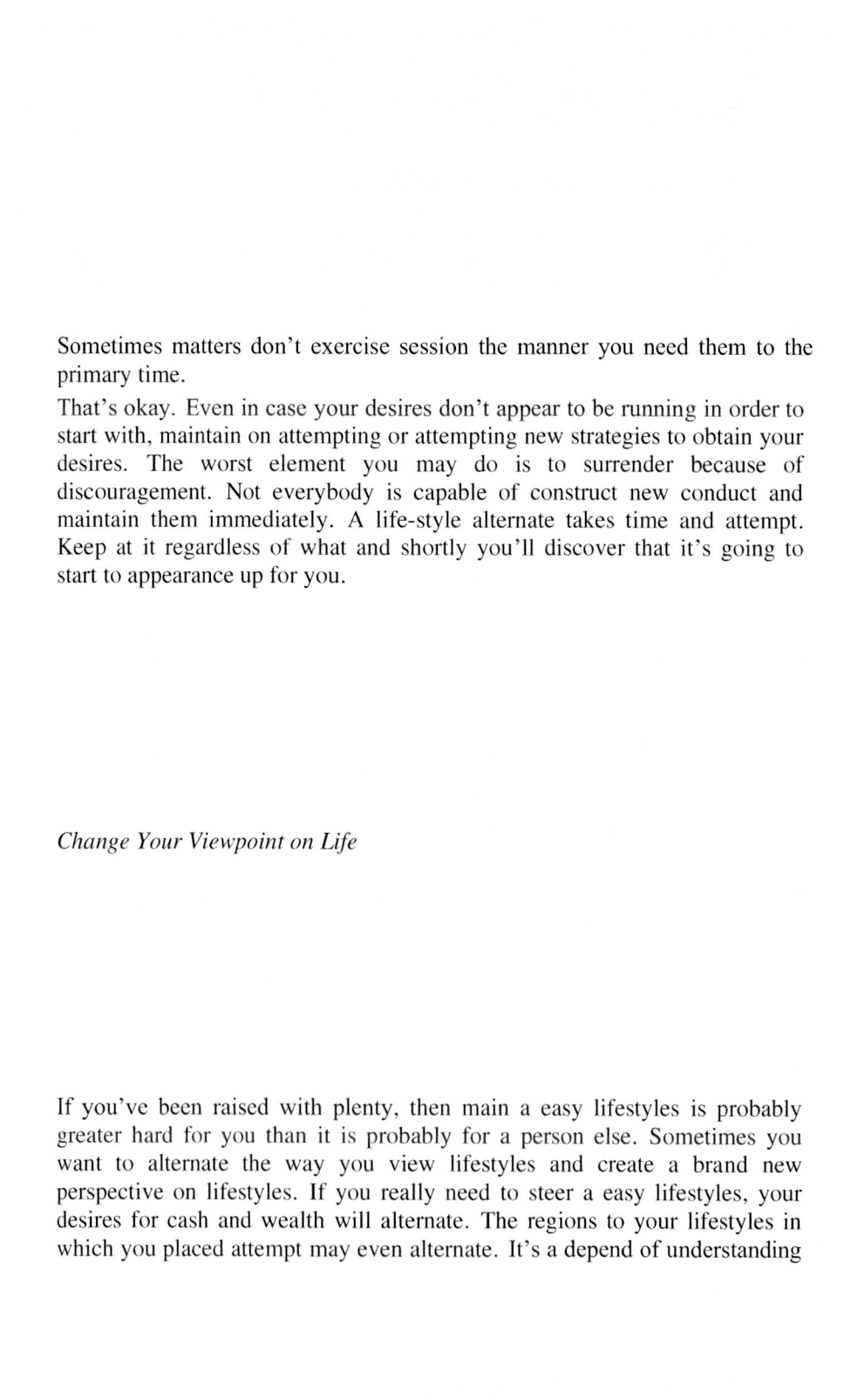

Sometimes matters don't exercise session the manner you need them to the primary time.

That's okay. Even in case your desires don't appear to be running in order to start with, maintain on attempting or attempting new strategies to obtain your desires. The worst element you may do is to surrender because of discouragement. Not everybody is capable of construct new conduct and maintain them immediately. A life-style alternate takes time and attempt. Keep at it regardless of what and shortly you'll discover that it's going to start to appearance up for you.

Change Your Viewpoint on Life

If you've been raised with plenty, then main a easy lifestyles is probably greater hard for you than it is probably for a person else. Sometimes you want to alternate the way you view lifestyles and create a brand new perspective on lifestyles. If you really need to steer a easy lifestyles, your desires for cash and wealth will alternate. The regions to your lifestyles in which you placed attempt may even alternate. It's a depend of understanding what's critical to you and maintain together along with your desires. Once you're capable of view your lifestyles via easy eyes, acquiring a easy lifestyle might be an awful lot less difficult.

Once you've got got a concrete machine to maintain your desires and easy life-style going, then preserving the life-style might be an awful lot less difficult to do. It won't manifest for you as speedy as you will like, however now no longer everybody can alternate their lives speedy. Keep striving in your desires and ensuring which you're seeking to view your lifestyles as easy while some thing complicated comes into the picture. Soon, you'll be residing a easy lifestyles and loving it!

Chapter 6- Enjoying More Time

Once you've got got the easy lifestyles going the manner which you need it, you'll discover that you'll have greater time to do what you revel in. When you understand what's critical and placed the relaxation aside, you'll recognise what having time is. Our lives have too many pulls upon our time, so understanding what's critical and setting them first will assist you to shed sports and possessions that aren't so critical. Everyone will discover exceptional layers of price of their lives, so what's critical to you'll now no longer always be critical to another.

Enjoying greater time will make it viable to position your critical movements and gadgets on the the front of your thoughts and lifestyles. Having much less you would possibly discover which you revel in greater. When you've got got a easy lifestyles, you'll discover which you won't omit the matters that used to appear too critical to you. You will start to discover greater price in what subjects maximum to your lifestyles. What could you do with greater time? What could you revel in doing?

Spending Time with Others

Everyone has someone or a collection of humans they revel in spending time with. Once you've got got a easy lifestyles, you'll have greater time to revel in the agency of these you need to be round. If you're nevertheless transitioning into this life-style, then you definitely won't even recognise what loose time is. Once you've got got the time to spend with the ones you care approximately, you'll love your easy lifestyles greater and greater. Life isn't approximately getting the maximum achieved however approximately spending it with humans we revel in and love.

Relaxing

Relaxation. What is that? This looks as if a dream that we are able to most effective get

while we ee-e book an extended vacation. However, periodic rest is ideal in your temper and your fitness. If you've got got time to easy take a seat down lower back and revel in the silence round you, examine a ee-e book, or do different sports you revel in, you'll experience happier and more healthy. The hassle with today's society is that we're all in one of these huge rush that no person even is aware of what enjoyable feels like. By taking up a easy life-style, having time to loosen up will experience good.

Lower Stress Levels

One of the maximum not unusualplace lawsuits of adults in our society is they experience careworn out. Why do they experience that manner? In a lifestyle that is making an attempt to get greater achieved in even much less time, quite a few strain rests on everybody's shoulders. However, the effects aren't even really well worth all of the pressure we placed into it. Stress is established to purpose fitness problems, takes away our focus, and some of different poor consequences. Some pressure is ideal to maintain us motivated, however an excessive amount of pressure is harmful. By taking up a easy lifestyles, you may shed quite a few the sports which have prompted you pressure and make your lifestyles more healthy and happier.

Better Health

As said on this chapter, residing a easy lifestyles will cause decrease pressure and greater time for relaxing. This is critical in keeping your health. If you've got got greater time on your day, you're capable of pursue sports that boom your health stages and pick out ingredients which might be more healthy and greater nutritious. When you've got got the time to assume thru your actions, you'll start to make selections which might be higher for you and your health.

Having greater time for your arms may be enjoyable. At first, you won't recognize a way to manage having time to do some thing you need, however after you get used to it, your down time turns into a necessity. I recognize I revel in my loose time. I get to spend time with others, do what I revel in doing, and my head feels tons clearer and I make higher selections.

I inspire you to strive the easy lifestyles. I had been residing it for approximately a yr now and sincerely love it. There is much less stress and I appearance and experience tons higher with out being run ragged and striving for fabric possessions. I desire you'll locate the identical leisure on your lifestyles.

Chapter 7- Enjoying the Simplicity of Life

Have you started to strive a number of the stairs on this ee-e book to try to lead a greater easy lifestyles? If you've got got, you may comprehend simply how tons you like having a easy lifestyles. The easy lifestyles with little is simply fuller than when you have a hectic lifestyles with many possessions. I love my easy lifestyles due to the fact I experience like it's now no longer cluttered and that I'm now no longer going for walks from one region to some other and by no means truely conducting anything. At the give up of the day, I experience comfortable and content material with myself and my lifestyles. What motives do you've got got for loving a easy lifestyles?

Our society performs upon doing greater and having greater. That is why it looks as if anyone runs from one region to some other with none regard to others. They simply need to get what they want carried out and anyone stands withinside the manner of that. However, once I locate that I even have greater and do greater, I am unhappy. I completed some thing, however it's now no longer what I need for myself. When I'm going for walks from region to region to ensure that my chore listing is finished earlier than the give up of the day, or I'm shopping for decorations for my outsized home, I'm now no longer truely playing the matters in my lifestyles that definitely count to me. I'm

genuinely a robotic this is residing as much as society's expectations.

Do you every now and then experience like a puppet? I love searching again at instances even fifty years in the past whilst lifestyles turned into tons much less complex and there has been tons greater cost to human beings as opposed to possessions. Life has modified lots withinside the beyond century. Let's face it, we handiest have a lot time upon this planet. For me, I might instead revel in it with what I revel in and love as opposed to residing as much as a social norm. Having wealth and popularity isn't always really well worth it if I'm now no longer going to be happy. We all need to be happy, so why now no longer so the matters so that it will make you happy?

Ever given that I started out to simplify my lifestyles, I even have discovered that spending time with my partner and my kids has end up tons greater critical. The children nevertheless revel in gambling sports, however the aggressive issue has been eliminated for them. If they need to play sports, this is their choice, now no longer some thing that I cause them to do due to the fact each different mom withinside the community has a baby at the team. I experience as aleven though they may be happier for it too. The pressure of acting nicely isn't always on their shoulders and they are able to play for amusing and now no longer fear approximately disappointing absolutely each person in the event that they lose. They genuinely deliver it their first-class efforts.

Once you understand what you need from your lifestyles and what's definitely critical to you, then you'll be nicely for your manner to creating your lifestyles simpler. Just due to the fact anyone else is doing it doesn't imply that it's miles the manner to happiness. I'm residing the easy lifestyles and loving it, and I desire that you could do the identical.

I desire you've got got received a few information from this ee-e book that you could positioned into exercise a number of the thoughts on this ee-e book into your lifestyles. The simplicity of lifestyles will make your lifestyles richer and fuller than looking to match greater in and having greater. Just cognizance on what's critical on your lifestyles.

Conclusion

Thank you once more for downloading this ee-e book!

I desire this ee-e book turned into capin a position that will help you to research a few treasured approaches to reduce down for your lifestyles so you can enjoy greater time. Once you locate which you reduce a number of the needless sports out of your lifestyles, you'll experience higher and revel in your lifestyles tons greater. Everyone desires to revel in lifestyles, so it's without a doubt really well worth a strive.

The subsequent step is to attempt to positioned a number of the stairs referred to on this ee-e book into action. Once you're capable of use the mind and thoughts mentioned on this ee-e book,

then you may discover that you may now no longer need as lots and feature greater. When I say greater, I suggest greater time and best time with the ones you care approximately. Give the thoughts in my ee-e book a attempt to see how the easy lifestyles can alternate the manner you stay and have a take a observe lifestyles!

Living Frugal and Loving It

Chapter 1: Looking on the Big Picture

With the fee of residing growing each year, there's no higher time than the prevailing to test your everyday lifestyles, and discover locations wherein you can be saving cash and decreasing waste. Below are a few easy suggestions with a view to assist get you started.

1. **Use less**

    While this will look like not unusualplace sense, a lot of us could be greatly surprised to recognise how lots we waste daily, in nearly each side of our lives. Most people should find the money for to apply much less in severa regions including: food, splendor products, gas, apparel, herbal resources, and different consumables. Think approximately enacting small modifications like looking to use much less toothpaste whilst you brush, or making sure which you use handiest sufficient laundry detergent to clean the weight length you've got got. For a lot of us our impulse appears to be greater is higher, and we don't even try and restrict ourselves while we have to. Try to take heed to your intake and your expenses will reduce.

2. **List your goals**

   It can show very useful in case you jot down a listing of your long-time period priorities, including saving for a house, or transforming a modern-day home. When you've got got set monetary dreams you're operating closer to, it's miles lots simpler to stay centered on saving cash to obtain that goal. Try to make certain that your financial savings are handiest going closer to those similarly out dreams, and now no longer being spent on short-tem dreams including vacations. If you've got got short-time period dreams you'd want to obtain, try and draw the cash from different regions of your budget,

   including leisure or ingesting out.

3. **Plan ahead**

   While this is straightforward sufficient to say, it could frequently show lots greater hard to implement. If you are making it a dependancy to suppose some distance earlier approximately what goes on to your lifestyles, you may in the long run store a giant quantity of cash. For example, in case you realize that you may be traveling, make certain to % a dinner or a lunch. If you discover your self unprepared you'll in all likelihood consume your meal at a restaurant (at an improved fee). If you understand which you'll be out all day, snatch a reusable bottle of water to keep away from paying extensively greater when you have to buy it. Is there an essential birthday coming up? Grab a present on sale earlier rather than scrambling the day of for the ideal gift.

4. **Look in advance for significant purchases**

   It is continually to your pleasant hobby to appearance earlier, and do your research, earlier than making any selections on a giant buy. For huge costs like home equipment or vehicles, hold your eyes peeled for sales, and don't be in a rush. Have a clean concept of what you need, and what a trendy fee is probably each new and used.

Often when you have patience, and a sturdy understanding of what some thing is worth, a deal can also additionally gift itself.

5. **Never buy things full price**

   While that is a rule you could't continually stick to, it's miles one which you have to continually goal for if in any respect feasible. If you want some thing take some time to investigate the usual fee and feasible sale prices, in addition to any reductions or coupons that could apply.

   Consider additionally your shopping for alternatives including on-line or in store. Try to shop for such things as apparel withinside the low season while objects are in all likelihood to be decreased to sell. Keep in thoughts that many shops could have a fee-fit policy, so understanding your stuff will make certain that you could

   take complete benefit of this choice.

6. **Re-evaluate your transportation**

   One of the greater giant expenses that a family can incur is that of proudly owning and working a vehicle. Between automobile payments, gas, insurance, and trendy maintenance, your automobile can frequently be a critical monetary drain. Why now no longer strive driving your bike, walking, or in case your town has it, using public transit? If you want a automobile you could continually lease one, and you'll probable nevertheless store hundreds of greenbacks a year. If announcing good-bye for your automobile isn't always an choice for you, discover the concept of carpooling. Carpooling permits a couple of human beings to percentage the fee of gas, parking, and different automobile-associated incidentals which could frequently upload up.

7. **Hand make your gifts**

While now no longer every body is an artist, with the proliferation of DIY on-line tutorials, and the social networking webweb page Pinterest, nearly everyone can whip up a innovative and considerate gift. Taking the time to make a present for a person now no longer most effective suggests a degree of care that they may appreciate, it'll regularly come to be saving you a tremendous quantity of cash.

8. **Consider used first**

   While it is able to be tempting to very own some thing vivid and new, used is continually a great choice to explore. When you're searching out a particular object, placed out feelers to look if everyone you know, or any in their connections, are promoting some thing similar. Ask around, ship out an email, or publish your request on a network board (both on-line or in excessive site visitors regions in which you live). You'll be amazed how regularly what you want it out there, and via way of means of accomplishing out, you're giving a person else a risk to remove some thing they'll now no longer need, at the same time as nonetheless getting what you want. If none of your direct contacts have what you're searching out, you may continually

   take a look at on-line webweb sites consisting of Craigslist or Freecycle, to look if there are any feasible deals there. A notable manner to do that is to have a jogging listing of gadgets which you are searching out, so you aren't simply specializing in one. Refer again to those webweb sites regularly to look if there are any new gadgets that capture your eye. If it isn't to your listing, don't purchase it! These webweb sites must be used to make you extra frugal, now no longer cause you shopping for extra stuff.

9. **Focus on increasing your income**

   While on-line webweb sites consisting of Craigslist or eBay may be notable assets whilst you are seeking to buy gadgets, they Also can convey you greater profits. Post gadgets you now no longer need which can have cost to a person else. You can regularly make a touch cash on matters you'll in any other case simply remove. Also, strive exploring whether or not you may choose up extra money via way of means of doing freelance or agreement paintings. Websites like oDesk and Elance will placed you in touch with customers who want paintings completed on a in step with process basis, which permits you to healthy it into your schedule. Take any greater profits you are making this manner and make sure which you placed it immediately into savings, in order that it doesn't get eaten up however non-crucial charges.

Chapter 2: Eating & Entertaining on a Budget

From exciting at home, to decreasing your meals invoice, there are numerous approaches to restriction your charges that don't need to suggest sacrificing the belongings you love. Look no similarly than your kitchen whilst you are looking for approaches to save.

10. **Eat out less**

One of the largest, maximum useless day by day prices that humans make, is ingesting outdoor of the home. The common character wastes over $2,000 a yr journeying fast-meals chains and eating in restaurants. This may be expensive, by no means thoughts awful on your health (which also can have long time results to your spending in case you turn out to be ill). It is continually less expensive to put together you very own meals. Try growing a weekly menu and sticking to it. It is essential that ingesting out turns into the exception, and now no longer the guideline of thumb on your household. If you do need to devour at a restaurant, strive some hints to be able to make certain your invoice doesn't wreck the bank. Skip the alcohol or smooth drinks, and rather ask for water. Water will fill you up and motive you to eat less, at the same time as additionally being free! Perhaps remember splitting a meal with a person, as maximum locations provide ridiculous, useless portions. You'll be searching after your health, and your wallet, and in case you experience stupid doing it, you've stored sufficient cash to reduce your embarrassment via way of means of giving the server a notable tip.

11. Cut coupons and look for vouchers Coupons and vouchers are a treasured device in a frugal character's arsenal. Check weekly flyers, clip coupons whilst you see them,
and seek on-line for codes and vouchers. Deals could be supplied in nearly each vicinity which you spend in, so hold your eyes peeled!

Know however, that at the same time as coupons and vouchers can prevent cash, it most effective works in case you buy matters which you normally
would. Don't clip coupons for luxurious gadgets which you wouldn't typically purchase. Coupons must help you with the necessities, now no longer upload every other purchasing object for your listing.

12. **Brown paper bag your lunches**

Absolutely every person has the cappotential to devise beforehand and % a lunch, and everyone who makes use of time constraints as an excuse isn't the use of their cash saving smarts. A packed or organized lunch will regularly price much less than $3, and take you just a few mins to throw together. In comparison, ingesting out or grabbing some thing quickly, will much more likely fall withinside the $7 - $20 range. This is one vicinity wherein humans are continuously careless, thoughtlessly reducing into their cash saving cappotential with the aid of using make hasty ingesting decisions.

13. **Cook ahead of time**

For many humans cooking every week or maybe a month earlier may be an first rate manner to shop cash. Plan a unfastened day wherein you may prepare dinner dinner meals in huge batches after which freeze them in dinner-sized potions. While this isn't some thing that humans can do all of the time, it is able to shop cash if applied even occasionally. There is a truthful quantity of making plans worried in this, however as soon as finished it's going to get rid of the every day meal making plans that regularly poses an difficulty for overworked and exhausted humans. Often while we're worn-out we revert to ingesting out or grabbing comfort meals, and having easy, to be had alternatives at domestic will at the least diminish that tendency.

14. Get a deep freeze

Investing in a huge freezer may be a high-quality manner to shop your self a few cash down the line. Lots of area will make sure that you may preplan your food earlier, in addition to purchase perishable gadgets in bulk. Try stocking up on sure meals while they're on sale, and hold them withinside the deep freeze till you want them. Reduced cuts of

meat, home made bread, and sparkling end result and veggies sold while in season, can all be properly saved withinside the freezer for destiny use. Knowing which you have a complete freezer of to be had alternatives also can be a consolation to humans throughout instances while cash isn't pretty as plentiful.

15. Search out affordable recipes

There are severa on-line webweb sites, in addition to specialised cookbooks, with a purpose to offer you with less costly, nutritious recipe alternatives.

Especially in case you are a beginner withinside the kitchen (however even in case you are not), those webweb sites and books can show invaluable. These reassets will regularly let you know on quite a few subjects which includes the exceptional, maximum less costly cuts of meat to apply in recipes, in addition to what's in season (and regularly priced lower) at sure instances of the year. Recipes may provide a standard price in keeping with portion, which may be useful records for humans looking to make higher monetary choices.

16. Grow and make your own food

Growing your very own lawn may be an first rate manner to reduce charges withinside the kitchen. Think of the veggies and herbs which you use maximum, and plant them withinside the spring, to gain the blessings withinside the summer. A lawn can yield a widespread quantity of meals, and an overabundance of it is able to usually be frozen or canned for later use. Explore additionally making your very own variations of meals you should buy withinside the store. Make your very own bread, strive dehydrating fruit, or appearance up recipes for sparkling home made variations of meals you may purchase premade, along with hummus or guacamole.

17. **Buy in bulk**

While many income and purchase-one-get-one-unfastened gives are designed to persuade you to shop for belongings you typically wouldn't, there are commonly some gadgets really well worth grabbing at a discounted rate. Be on the

lookout for income and specials on non-perishable gadgets which you regularly want along with canned goods, pasta, and rice. These are gadgets which you realize you'll finally use, so if you may discover a bargain inventory up. Only purchase in bulk for those forms of requirements or you can come to be with gadgets you don't need or want.

18. **Have a concept of the average prices for common goods**

Being organized and doing all of your homework is a primary factor of staying thrifty whilst you are grocery purchasing. Do a bit detective paintings earlier than you head out and examine the price of meals staples at exclusive shops to be had to you. See if you may deduce any traits withinside the gadgets which can be commonly extra less costly at every store. You can also additionally come to be having more than one grocery shops that every provide some thing which you need. For instance one can be commonly the maximum less costly, even as some other can also additionally have the exceptional fees for meat or produce. Try to prepare you grocery purchasing to make sure which you have become what you want from every store. If you don't have a strong idea of what a median rate is, you depart your self prone to purchases that can be drastically extra than you'll have paid elsewhere.

19. **Make your own alcohol**

If you entertain regularly, or in case you experience a tumbler of wine or a chilly beer, it is able to frequently be very price green in an effort to inspect making your very own alcohol. While there's a few price for set-up in case you are making it from your very own residence, it's going to fast be absorbed whilst you understand you're stocking your wine cellar and beer refrigerator for a fragment of what you'll pay in shops. If you want the rate factor however aren't inclined to do all of the work, there are numerous make your very own wine and beer centers to help you with the process, even as nonetheless supplying a appreciably decrease price consistent with bottle.

20. **Entertain your friends at home**

Are you a social butterfly who loves spending pleasant time together along with your pals, however doesn't always have the finances for dinner and liquids at the town? Why now no longer attempting web website hosting a night-in at your place, in which humans can every carry a extraordinary snack or potluck dish, and you may arrange video games or a film viewing? This can also additionally require a touch greater making plans than a journey to a restaurant, however your pockets will gain the benefits. Keep in thoughts that in case you are making plans a celebration in which an invite is required, you may use on-line offerings like Evite to take gain of unfastened, or low-price alternatives. If you want substances together with napkins, cups, or plates, inventory up whilst you see them on sale, or hit up your neighborhood greenback store. Spending time together along with your pals doesn't ought to imply spending heaps of coins.

21. **Drink more water.**

This one appears easy due to the fact it's far. Water is fresh and hydrating, or even greater importantly to the frugal – it's unfastened! Cut out alcohol, gentle liquids, coffee, tea and juices, and you'll discover at once which you have a touch more money for your pocket.

Chapter 3: Health & Beauty Hacks to Save Money

While maintaining ourselves searching and feeling excellent is crucial, there are methods that we are able to make certain that we're nonetheless being financially conscious, and looking our consumption. While you don't ought to scrimp, right here are some beneficial pointers on a way to store a touch coins even as nonetheless looking after yourself.

22. Don't purchase call logo over-the-counter remedy For many not unusualplace medicines together with ache relievers or anti- histamines, the elements are honestly same whilst you evaluate call logo and regular. Check bulk shops for big bottles of the medicines you use, and while there's a desire, choose the residence logo. There is surely no distinction in how they'll work. Also, attempt looking on-line for a more desire of regular manufacturers that can be even greater affordable. Often you may rating a tremendous deal simply through purchasing round and checking your alternatives.

23. **Ditch the gym**

For many humans a health clubnasium club is some thing they underutilize on the great of times, even as for others it's far a whole waste of cash. Regardless of whether or not you employ a club or now no longer, recognize that there are numerous different alternatives for maintaining match that you may probe for a fragment of the price of the health clubnasium. Walk, run, cycle, or simply get outside! If you'd instead stick near home, inspect the severa on-line sources that provide unfastened yoga, health, and dance classes (amongst different alternatives). There are methods to maintain match that don't have to interrupt the bank. Remember though, even as we don't recommend you shell out a ton of cash at the health clubnasium, maintain in thoughts that preserving your bodily health is an

funding you have to make. When you attention on preventative care you're making sure a destiny now no longer slowed down through bad fitness and the monetary troubles that frequently accompany it.

24. **Good to the last drop**

While lots of us want to faux that we're notable acutely aware of losing our sources, we frequently act pretty carelessly with matters that price us cash. We can also additionally casually toss a now no longer pretty empty toothpaste due to the fact we are able to't get it from the lowest of the tube, or throw out a moisturizer as it doesn't pop out with pretty the identical amount as earlier than. In order to be thrifty it's far crucial to make certain that we're the use of the whole lot to the remaining drop. We can do that through slicing up tubes and emptying them absolutely earlier than we throw them away.

Chapter 4: Checking Your Financial Fitness

Being financially withinside the recognize may be liberating, and having a strong draw close on in which to cut, and in which to store, can sincerely assist you in your direction to monetary freedom. Keep a near eye in your finances and employ the guidelines below.

25. **Bank smarter**

Banking smarter way making any wide variety of small adjustments in order to boom the quantity of cash which you are saving. A notable manner to get began out is via way of means of switching your financial institution account over to a issuer who gives no-price accounts. There isn't anyt any purpose you need to be paying renovation or utilization fees, so locate a person who will provide you an alternative. Try additionally to peer if you could negotiate credit score card or mortgage hobby quotes with you financial institution. It by no means hurts to ask, and frequently you may receive! Banking is a aggressive business, so in the event that they can't provide you a deal that makes you happy, appearance elsewhere. Keep in thoughts though, that one surefire manner to store your self cash is via way of means of decreasing any useless credit score you will be paying hobby on. Have a credit score card if it's far truly necessary, however maintain the stability low, or pay it off month-to-month to make certain which you aren't losing bucks that might be going elsewhere.

26. **Have an automatic savings plan**

A notable manner to begin flexing your frugality muscular tissues is via way of means of shifting cash robotically off of your paychecks. Put this cash without delay right into a financial savings account, and remember it now no longer a part of the cash you could spend. We have a tendency to try and stay to whatever way we have, so frequently larger paychecks simply way greater spending. Remove the extra money from the equation and spot what you could make due with. 20% is a notable beginning point, however examine how that works for you and boom or lower accordingly. If you don't see the cash, possibilities are you won't pass over it. The simplest stipulation to this rule is in case you are wearing considerable debt. If that is the case simplest have a small emergency financial savings fund, as you need to be allocating cash to debt, that's a severe cash drain which you need to try and remove.

27. Use a rewards credit card

While the simply frugal might advise for no credit score, rewards credit score playing cards may be a notable alternative for the ones who've a stable cope with on their spending. Often new playing cards will provide sign-up bonuses in coins, air miles, or points. If you could take benefit of those responsibly, and now no longer boom your intake at all, this could be a notable benefit. This is largely more money which you wouldn't have had otherwise. Using your rewards playing cards to pay for the whole lot, which includes bills, will assist you amass advantages which you wouldn't with a debit card. This can simplest paintings in case you spend responsibly though. Running up a credit score card to get air miles doesn't paintings in case you are spending masses each month in hobby.

Chapter 5: Targeting the Technology Cash Drain

We stay in a global ruled via way of means of generation, and for lots of us it's far an absolute necessity. Take a while but to remember if there are any technological conveniences you could reduce or lessen to store your self a few bucks.

28. Limit your devices

While it is able to be amusing to have all of the new devices that muddle the market, try and absolutely remember what you want generation wise. If your process calls for you to write down briefs or create complicated presentations, then a computer can be necessary. If but, you become the usage of your computer in basic terms to surf the internet or test emails, you would possibly remember simply having a clever telecellsmartphone that does the whole lot you want at a discounted fee. Many human beings additionally have move over withinside the gadgets that they own, proudly owning a couple of gadgets that do the identical things. One individual doesn't want an IPod, IPhone, IPad and Mac computer, however it's far very probably that many human beings own all of those things. Try to absolutely examine your wishes and downsize while now no longer necessary.

29. Cut your cable

Gone are the times while cable tv linked you to the whole lot that became occurring withinside the global. With the arrival of on line webweb sites wherein you could view absolutely whatever you need, and the appearance of very low fee subscription packages, cable is now no longer a need for lots households. Save a few coins via way of means of downsizing or disposing of an steeply-priced package, and choose and select what you need from less costly on line options. Often cable results in infinite channel surfing, and killing time looking belongings you aren't absolutely involved in. A effective aspect impact of ditching it's far that you could simplest become looking tv for specific

programs, main to much less time wasted at the couch.

30. Negotiate with your providers

Many corporations that offer offerings like telecellsmartphone and net service, can have the funds for to be greater bendy than they might have you ever believe. Just due to the fact they gift you with a price, doesn't imply this is the very last provide. Don't be afraid to name customer support and allow them to recognise which you are exploring different options. Check in with them each few months and notice what new offers they're presenting to new clients. Once they've already secured your commercial enterprise they actually won't be calling you to lessen your bill, however if they could provide to new people, they ought to be capable of provide it to you. It by no means hurts to ask, and regularly you may stable a few remarkable offers.

Chapter 6: Don't be House Poor

Your domestic is your palace, and for a lot of us (specifically the ones looking to reduce lower back on costs) it's miles wherein we spend the bulk of our time. Ensure that your property isn't a drain for your budget through following the hints under.

31. Get the house you NEED, not the house you WANT

In the aggressive housing marketplace banks regularly attempt to provide exceptionally low hobby prices and excessive loan approvals to trap buyers. Just due to the fact you're permitted for a $500,000 loan, doesn't imply you need to take it. Think critically approximately what kind of residence possesses all the belongings you need, with out veering too a ways into what you need on pinnacle of that. You can be capable of discover a residence for $200,000 that suits all your criteria, so don't be tempted through the greater high-priced residence. While it could be nicer, if the opposite residence suits your conditions, there may be no logical motive to pay greater. Keep in thoughts which you might imagine you may have the funds for a bigger loan, however whilst you aspect in utilities, belongings taxes, upkeep, and surprising incidentals in an effort to arise, you'll be in for greater than you bargained for.

32. Ensure the efficiency of your home

Your domestic can regularly be one of the important cash drains for your life. While a few matters are past your control, there are some matters you may do to make sure that your private home isn't siphoning cash at once out of your savings. First, make sure that it's miles nicely insulated. This can encompass checking for any locations that warmth would possibly break out from, and home windows are regularly a key culprit. Make positive that home windows aren't a warmth drain, and update something that threatens to hike up your bills. If you may't have the funds for to update home windows you may cowl them with plastic withinside the cooler months to maintain heat air

from escaping and cooler air getting in. Also, make sure which you are the use of home equipment and energy wisely. Turn off lighting whilst you depart a room, and attempt now no longer to apply water for washing or dishwashing all through height hours. Finally, attempt now no longer to mess around an excessive amount of together along with your thermostat. Even shifting it through some stages can critically have an effect on your software bills. Throw on a sweater or spend money on a couple of slippers, and your financial institution account will thank you.

33. Make your own cleaning products

While grocery store cleansing merchandise can regularly fee a premium, a short appearance for your cabinets may also provide you a mess of elements that also can do the trick, at a fragment of the price. Try the use of a teaspoon of bicarbonate of soda on a humid material to imitate a cream cleanser. White vinegar is likewise an exceptional all-cause component whether or not you're washing your home windows or cleansing your floors. There is sincerely no motive to pay excessive fees for brand-call gadgets whilst you may do a short seek at the net in an effort to screen severa cleansing product recipes in an effort to prevent cash, and maintain your private home spotless.

34. Master the art of DIY

While there are a few matters, like plumbing and electrical, which ought to be left to professionals, there are numerous do-it-your self hints that you may hire to keep your self a few cash. Online tutorials in the way to do small maintenance round your property make venture family tasks that an awful lot easier. You also can go to your large hardware shops for records on tasks like tiling and painting. When you restoration some thing your self, you now no longer best advantage a extreme feel of accomplishment, you furthermore mght keep cash!

Chapter 7: Looking Good For Less

While it could be a laugh to have new clothes, that is a first-rate place of expenditure for numerous people, and one of the maximum apparent locations that you may make adjustments for the better. Consider those hints under earlier than shopping for new, or tossing the old.

35. Wash clothes less

While a few humans put on garments as soon as after which throw them withinside the wash, this isn't always the first-rate manner to preserve the shade and exceptional of your gadgets. Unless you've got got a process which includes your garments getting extraordinarily grimy, otherwise you hit the fitness center and sweat profusely, maximum garments may be worn greater than as soon as earlier than tossing them withinside the wash. Use the odor check to infer whether or not they're in reality grimy or not. You'll recognize proper away if they are able to stick round for every other put on, or if it's time to position them withinside the hamper. This can prevent cash on washing, however it'll additionally serve to increase the lifestyles of your garb.

36. Hang-dry clothes

While dryers are fast, they aren't continually the first-rate alternative in case you are seeking to lessen electricity utilization and lengthen the lifestyles of your garb. Especially in case you are doing smaller loads, take a couple of minutes to dangle them up. If the solar is shining they'll be dry earlier than you realize it, however even drying on racks interior may be higher to your gadgets and shop your strength bills. Air-drying manner that not anything is being shriveled or damaged, and this will prevent even extra cash ultimately whilst you don't have to shop for new garments.

37. Shop at consignment boutiques

Clothing purchasing is every other place wherein you may choose to shop for used. Visit consignment stores wherein you may frequently locate amazing gadgets at a significantly decreased rate. In fact, many gadgets will be

slightly used, and when you have staying power you have to be capable of land your self some super portions. When purchasing antique you may additionally raid your parents' or grandparents' antique closets for portions from preceding decades. You can hit on a few genuinely lovely gadgets that can be the peak of favor this manner. Don't permit snobbery or distaste for second-hand, prevent you from locating exquisite bargains.

38. Spend money on quality

While it frequently appears counterintuitive whilst you are attempting to be frugal, it's far frequently sensible to pay extra cash for garb than less. Often inexpensive gadgets are low exceptional and won't be capable of preserve out lengthy sufficient with a purpose to refresh them or lengthen their lifestyles. High exceptional gadgets can also additionally include a better rate tag, however attempt to think about them as investments. Buy staples that you may put on for years, in place of disposable garb that won't ultimate a season. Evaluate the exceptional of garb via way of means of checking the sewing for free threads, and make certain that any styles healthy up. Try additionally bunching the cloth on your hand for some seconds after which watch if it returns to its herbal shape. Make clever style selections and also you have to have amazing gadgets for greater than lengthy sufficient to justify the cost.

39. Take care of your clothes

While everyday put on and tear is unavoidable, you may frequently lengthen the lifestyles of your garb with some easy steps. Instead of throwing away fuzzy sweaters use a razor blade to do away with pilling and refresh the wool. Try additionally death dwindled jeans, or digging out the stitching device to restore any garb with lacking buttons or small holes. If you're bored of what's on your closet, attempt to get innovative via way of means of bringing new lifestyles to antique gadgets. Head to markets or stitching stores and locate creative elements to jazz up worn-out antique apparel. Check style magazines and net pics for inspiration, and make it your own!

40. Host a clothing swap

A garb switch may be a super manner to dispose of gadgets you not need, at the same time as obtaining new ones at no cost! Ask your girlfriends to undergo their closets and produce gadgets they need to dispose of. Have them carry the whole thing to a get-collectively wherein absolutely each person receives to kind thru and choose out the gadgets they like.

Throw in a few appetizers and wine and also you've were given a party! This concept also can be prolonged to encompass children's garb, when you have a set of moms with youngsters of differing ages.

Conclusion

Thank you once more for downloading this ee-e book!

I wish this ee-e book become capable of assist encourage you to right now begin searching on the approaches wherein you may restriction consumption, and shop cash on your day by day lifestyles.

The subsequent step is to domesticate a aware attention of the approaches wherein you may employ the guidelines and hints on this ee-e book, making sure your self the economic freedom and safety you desire.

Thank you and excellent luck!

Printed in Great Britain
by Amazon